Advance
Your English

A short course for advanced learners

Workbook

Annie Broadhead

CAMBRIDGE
UNIVERSITY PRESS

PUBLISHED BY THE PRESS SYNDICATE OF THE UNIVERSITY OF CAMBRIDGE
The Pitt Building, Trumpington Street, Cambridge, United Kingdom

CAMBRIDGE UNIVERSITY PRESS
The Edinburgh Building, Cambridge CB2 2RU, UK
40 West 20th Street, New York, NY 10011–4211, USA
10 Stamford Road, Oakleigh, VIC 3166, Australia
Ruiz de Alarcón 13, 28014 Madrid, Spain
Dock House, The Waterfront, Cape Town 8001, South Africa

http://www.cambridge.org

First published 2000
Third printing 2001

Printed in the United Kingdom at the University Press, Cambridge

Produced by Gecko Ltd, Bicester, Oxon

Typeface Formata Condensed 9.75/12pt   *System* QuarkXPress®

ISBN 0 521 59779 X   Coursebook
ISBN 0 521 59778 1   Teacher's Book
ISBN 0 521 59777 3   Class Cassette
ISBN 0 521 59776 5   Workbook
ISBN 0 521 59775 7   Workbook Cassette

Contents

Introduction

About this book

This Workbook is designed for use in conjunction with the *Advance Your English* Coursebook. It offers further practice and consolidation of the material in the Coursebook and, in some cases, development of Coursebook work.

Accompanied by its own cassette, the Workbook runs parallel to the Coursebook with 13 main units and three review units (Units 5, 10 and 16). The review units in the Workbook take the form of tests for self-assessment. These will help you check your progress.

A special feature at the end of most Workbook units is *Reading for pleasure* or *Listening for pleasure*. This is literally what it says – a text or recording which is to be enjoyed. There is no exercise or activity arising from it.

How to use this book

You can use the Workbook independently, as full answers and tapescripts are included, or it can be used as additional classroom material.

If you are working independently, you can either do the Workbook unit at the same time as the Coursebook unit or you may prefer to do the Workbook units later. Both methods have their advantages. Working in tandem with the Coursebook allows you to explore the topic more fully using related material; working after the Coursebook units will enable you to recycle what you have learnt and check how much you can remember.

Depending on how much time you have available, you can work through the whole of each Workbook unit or simply choose those areas where you would like more practice. Try to complete the tasks and exercises in the Workbook without referring to the Coursebook or answers first. Then check your answers carefully. If they are incorrect, make a note of your mistake(s) and go back and read the question again to try to understand what went wrong. Then have another look at the appropriate unit of the Coursebook. If necessary, consult a teacher about any points which still cause problems. Of course, when the answers are right, it means you have understood the Coursebook and the Workbook task and are coping well with related material.

When you are using the Workbook, you will find a good English–English dictionary, such as *Cambridge International Dictionary of English* (Cambridge University Press 1995), and a good grammar book, for example *Advanced Grammar in Use* by Martin Hewings (Cambridge University Press 1999), helpful.

Key to symbols

cassette-based tasks and tapescripts

answers on pages 46–60

Acknowledgements

Author's acknowledgements

The author would like to thank colleagues at EF International Language School, Cambridge, in particular, Fiona Fallon, Jo Philips and Jill Stewart for their support. Special thanks to my editors, Charlotte Adams, Niki Browne and Erica Hall, who all gave invaluable help and support. On the home front, thanks to Robbie Burns for computer support and lots more.

The author and publishers would like to thank the following teachers and advisors who trialled and commented on the material and whose feedback was invaluable.

Mark Appleby, Spain; Anna-Marie Burke, UK; Henny Burke, Spain; Philip Devlin, Germany; Romayne Grangereau, France; Gökhan Gültek, Turkey; Jane Hann, UK; Joanne Lenthall, UK; Deirdre Mulrennan, Italy; Patricia O'Sullivan, UK; Aytül Özer, Turkey; Sandra Possas, Brazil; R S Pryor, UK; Roger Scott, UK; Mira Shapur, UK; Peter Watkins, UK; Clare West, UK.

The author and publishers are grateful to the following for permission to reproduce copyright material. It has not always been possible to identify the sources of all the material used and in such cases the publishers would welcome information from the copyright owners. Apologies are expressed for any omissions.

p. 2: Rachel Kelly for 'At home in an office of my own' © Times Newspapers Limited; p. 5: Nigel Hawkes for 'The shopper always turns right' © Times Newspapers Limited; p. 6: listening text adapted from *The Cambridge Encyclopedia of the English Language* (1995) by David Crystal © Cambridge University Press; p. 6: Robin Young for 'This story should be read from left to right' © Times Newspapers Limited; p. 8: © Joe Roberts/Times Newspapers Limited for 'A brush with Gauguin's Nature World'; p. 9: Katherine Pierpoint for the poem 'Swim right up to me' published by Faber and Faber; p. 9: notices taken from Gerard Hoffnung's speech at the Oxford Union in 1958 with the kind permission of Annetta Hoffnung; p. 11: Liz Hollis for the listening text based on 'Mood food' from *Healthy Eating*; pp. 11–12 *Focus* for 'What's so good about bug grub?'; p. 15: Joanna Trollope for the extract from *A Spanish Lover*. Reprinted by permission of the Peters Fraser & Dunlop Group Ltd; p. 17: © Lisa Jardine/Times Newspapers Limited; p. 20: 'Rich pickings' © Sue Reid/ Times Newspapers Limited; p. 21: © Cash Peters and Loveday Miller. Extracted from *The Tell Tale Alphabet* by Cash Peters with Loveday Miller, published by Corgi, a division of Transworld Publishers. All rights reserved; p. 23: Yevgeny Yevtushenko for the poem 'Colours'; p. 24: *The Guardian*/Duncan Campbell for 'Latino girls shake up the field'; p. 26 *The Independent*/Kim Sengupta; p. 27: Anjana Ahuyja/*The Times*; p. 29: 'I have always got even' © Barry Wigmore/*The Times*; p. 32: *The Real Meaning of Money* © Dorothy Rowe 1997. Reprinted by kind permission of the author and the Lisa Eveleigh Literary Agency; p. 33: *The Independent* for the listening text based on 'Terminal Five at Heathrow: as certain as the global crisis it will help to encourage' by Polly Toynbee; p. 34: *The Independent* for 'Less of your lip: A history of the kiss'; p. 36: listening text adapted from *The Science of Sod's Law*, based on the research and writings of Robert A J Matthews; p. 38: Chris Barrie; p. 39: Tamagotchi article © 1997 *The Washington Post*. Reprinted with kind permission; p. 40: 'How to pack a suitcase' © Mark Hodson/Times Newspapers Limited; p. 41 Stanton Newman and Susan Londale for 'Personal Space' from *Human Jungle* © Ebury; p. 43: limericks and artwork taken from *Explosion of Limericks*, Holland Cassell (now part of Orion Publishing Group).

The author and publishers are grateful to the following illustrators and photographic sources.

Illustrators:

Kathy Baxendale, Phil Healey, John Storey, Peter Visscher and Gecko Ltd.

Photographic sources:

Photograph on p. 2 of home worker: Tony Stone Images/Frank Herholdt; photograph on p. 4 of shopper: Tony Stone Images/Jon Gray; photograph on p. 5 of supermarket: Tony Stone Images/Rex Butcher; photograph on p. 7 of Ghandi: Superstock; Gauguin photograph on p. 8: Superstock; photograph on p. 11 of food: Trevor Clifford; photograph on p. 12 of edible food: Corbis-Sygma/ S Cardinale; photograph on p. 12 of cricket: Tony Stone Images/Robert Holmgren; photograph on p. 12 of caterpillar: Tony Stone Images; photograph of book on p. 15: Transworld Publishers Ltd/Trevor Clifford; photograph on p. 20 of dining room: Robert Harding Picture Library; photograph on p. 22 of commuters: Tony Stone Images/David Oliver; photograph on p. 26 of Tracy Edwards: Katz Pictures/Tom Stoddart; photograph on p. 32 of money: Tony Stone Images/Olney Vasan; photograph on p. 33 of airport; Sygma/M Polak; photograph on p. 34 of The Kiss by Gustav Klimt: The Bridgeman Art Library.

Freelance picture research by Diane Jones.

Book design by Nick Newton and Dave Seabourne.

Produced by Gecko Ltd, Bicester, Oxon.

Cover design by Mark Diaper.

The cassette which accompanies this book was produced by Martin Williamson, Prolingua Productions at Studio AVP, London.

1

1 VOCABULARY
Abbreviations

Academic achievement is often judged by the number and type of qualifications someone has. We often use abbreviations to refer to people's educational qualifications.

a 🗝 **What do these British educational qualifications mean?**

1 A levels
2 MA   MSc   MBA
3 GCSE
4 BA   BSc
5 PhD

b 🗝 **Put the qualifications in a in order, starting with the highest.**

c 🗝 **Complete these sentences using the abbreviations in the list. What do the abbreviations stand for? Use a dictionary for any which you do not know.**

DIY   Euro MP   GP   HQ   IQ
PA   PC   PM   VAT   VIP

1 The sound on the new .... system is much clearer.
2 Have you seen your .... yet about your sore knee?
3 She spends a lot of time in Brussels now that she's our ....
4 You can't book Major Burlington into that little guest house; he'll expect .... treatment.
5 I hope .... doesn't go up in this year's budget.
6 That hammering is driving me mad. I'll be glad when the neighbour's .... projects come to an end.
7 The .... is making more public appearances in the run up to the election.
8 I think the bank's .... is in New York.
9 I only bought this .... a year ago, and it has already been superseded by a better model with a larger memory.
10 I took an .... test the other day. I'm not sure I want the results!

2 GRAMMAR Infinitive or *-ing* form?

a 🗝 **Divide these verbs into two groups – those which are followed by the infinitive and those which are followed by the *-ing* form.**

agree	appear	avoid	beg	decide	deny	expect
fancy	give up	hope	manage	mind	offer	permit
persuade	practise	pretend	refuse	risk	suggest	

b 🗝 **In this letter from a travel agent to an English-speaking customer, the writer has used the *-ing* form incorrectly eight times. She has also used the wrong preposition three times and the wrong word five times. Can you correct the mistakes? The first one has been done for you.**

Dear Mr Burns

I am very pleased ~~confirming~~ *to confirm* your forthcoming travel arrangements and, with regard to this matter, enclose your invoice and financial statement. I trust you will find these being in order, but do not hesitate contacting me should you have any queries or concerns.

As settlement was made to full by the time of booking, no more payment is due.

If you are travelling abroad, it is your responsibility ensuring that you and all candidates of your party have a worthy passport and any necessary visas. If you are of any doubt, please do not hesitate contacting me.

We shall of course be delighted supplying your foreign exchange requirements and helping you with any queries you may have relating to car hire, airport hotel accommodation and airport car parking.

May I take this occasion of thanking you once again for booking with Worldwide Tours.

Yours faithfully

C. Garcia

C. Garcia

Encs: invoice
         financial statement

3 READING

a 🔑 Read this article about working at home rather than travelling to a place of work every day. Six sentences have been removed from the article. Choose from sentences A–F the one which fits each gap (1–6). The first one has been done for you.

A 'Many of the problems faced by towns and cities are the legacy of previous working patterns,' Sir Terence says.
B The answer should be to create 'mixed use' communities, Sir Terence says.
C Sir Terence takes the argument further still.
D Today the trend towards working from home is growing.
E Simon Langford, of *Home Run* magazine, says that working from home can solve the problems of more traditional office life.
F It was the Victorians, he points out, who began the sharp division between home and work.

At home in an office of my own

The man who campaigned for cheap and stylish furniture and gave us Habitat is banging the drum again – this
5 time on the need to integrate social and working life, the 'ultimate challenge for design in the area of work'.

In his new book, Terence
10 Conran on Design, he argues that many urban problems have been created by the separation between home and work.

[1] [F] 'When the head of the household crossed the threshold of his
15 home at the end of the working day, he entered a cosy domain stuffed with curios and swathed with fabric and trimmings that obliterated any outward sign of function, an environment as different as possible from the workplace.' The home was intended as a refuge from work, and a place to display the status symbols that wages could buy.

20 [2] [ ] In Britain nearly 700,000 do so. In America 12 million people are based at home full-time.

[3] [ ] 'Many commuters face a ghastly journey to the office every day. Train strikes and poor weather conditions make things worse. Working from home avoids this, and can increase productivity for an employer by up
25 to 40 per cent, as well as saving costs and reducing stress for employees.'

[4] [ ] The very fabric of our cities could change thanks to the fact that work need no longer be tied to the workplace, be it office block, factory or out-of-town industrial park. Here is a real chance to redefine urban space, he argues.

30 [5] [ ] 'The dormitory village, the commuter town, the featureless suburb as much as the urban slum are the products of a rigid compartmentalisation of working life and social life. The effect has been to knock the heart out of many cities and create satellite communities with no sense of vitality.'

[6] [ ] Shops, workplaces, schools and leisure facilities should exist side
35 by side, creating a 'tight bustling network and more community-based life'.

b 🔑 Explain in your own words these words and phrases as they are used in the article.

1 the head of the household (line 14)
2 crossed the threshold of (line 14)
3 a cosy domain (line 15)
4 swathed with fabric and trimmings (line 16)
5 obliterated any outward sign of function (lines 16–17)
6 to display the status symbols (lines 18–19)
7 commuters (line 22)
8 the very fabric of our cities (line 26)
9 dormitory village (line 30)
10 featureless suburb (line 30)
11 urban slum (line 31)

4 VOCABULARY Words connected with work

a 🔑 Using an English–English dictionary, look up the meaning of the underlined words and phrases in these sentences.

1 He's been <u>on the dole</u> for six months.
2 I'll have to do a <u>crash course</u> in Spanish before I take the job.
3 She's a <u>freelance</u> journalist.
4 I was surprised the <u>probationary period</u> is only six months. I'll soon know if they will take me on permanently.
5 The company is radically <u>downsizing</u>. Bad news for lots of employees.
6 Working <u>flexitime</u> is wonderful. I no longer sit in a traffic jam every morning.
7 He was made <u>redundant</u> at the end of last year.
8 She has a real <u>flair</u> for that branch of law.
9 Computer time is paid for <u>pro rata</u>.
10 A lot of top level stockbrokers are <u>burnt out</u> by the time they are 30.
11 I really feel that would be paying <u>over the odds</u>.
12 What's the <u>going rate</u> for a two-year-old Mercedes?

b Choose six of the words or phrases which you might find difficult to remember and use them to write six sentences or a paragraph of your own.

5 LISTENING

a [icons] You will hear four people talking about their jobs. Listen and number the jobs in the order you hear them. Which two jobs are not mentioned?

chemist □
TV newsreader □
doctor □
engineer □
lawyer □
banker □

b [icons] Listen again and write down the key words connected with the person's job, e.g. the key words connected with a doctor might be: *patient*, *surgery*, *prescription*.

c [icons] Listen a third time and choose a mood from the list for each speaker.

bitter   incredulous   resigned   amused
indignant   embarrassed

6 PRONUNCIATION Long vowels

a [icon] Listen and repeat these words, paying particular attention to the vowel sound.

street /iː/
start /ɑː/
walk /ɔː/
shoes /uː/
terminus /ɜː/

b [icons] You are going to play *Stepping stones*. As in the Coursebook, the object of the game is to cross the river using the words as 'stepping stones'. You are allowed to step vertically or diagonally. Here you can move to the next stepping stone by choosing a word with the *same long vowel sound* in the *stressed syllable*. There are five routes across the river. In each line there are two words which do not contain a long vowel.

First mark the stressed syllable of each word. Listen and check your answers, then find the five routes across the river.

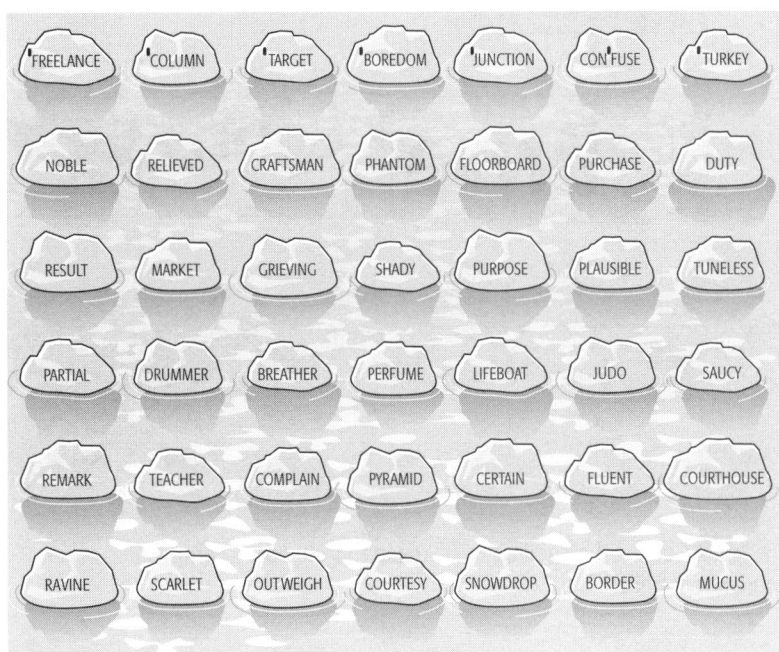

7 READING FOR PLEASURE

ODE TO WORK

I AM TIRED BECAUSE I AM OVERWORKED
The population of Britain is **51** million. **21** million are retired.
That leaves **30** million to do the work.
There are **19** million in school.
That leaves **11** million to do the work.
Of this total, **2** million are unemployed and **4** million are employed by the government.
That leaves **5** million to do the work.
1 million are in the armed forces

Which leaves **4** million to do the work!
From that total **3** million are employed by the County and Borough Councils
Leaving **1** million to do the work!
There are **620,000** people in hospitals and **379,998** in prison
That leaves **2** people to do the work!
You and **me**.
And you are sitting doing nothing reading this …
NO WONDER I AM TIRED!!!

2

1 VOCABULARY Spelling

a 🖾 Words are often spelt 'incorrectly' in advertising in order to catch our attention. What do these notices or names mean and how should they be spelt?

1

2

3

4

5

6

7

8

9

10

b 🖾 Correct the spelling mistakes in this student's composition on 'shopaholics'.

I supose a shopoholic is someone whose life revolves around shopping; it's central to thier live and starts to push out all other normal aktivities. These peope, if they are not actualy shopping, are anscious and woried or full of excitment based on the next day's shopping. Secondly, and probablly the most significent indicater of a shopaholic, is when people don't actualy get any plesure from the goods after they've bought them. Onse they leave the shop, they may never touch the goods; they hide them awaye. And, of cource, most people carry on despite the growing negativ consequenses of credit card det.

2 READING

a 🖉 Read this article about shopping and the things supermarkets do to make us buy more. Which paragraph in the article is about:

1 the layout of supermarkets?
2 shopping becoming a hobby?
3 entrance psychology?
4 the different types of shopper?
5 the atmosphere supermarkets create?
6 controlling the flow of shoppers?

THE SHOPPER ALWAYS TURNS RIGHT

To those of us for whom shopping is a chore, it seems perverse actually to enjoy it. But shopping, the market researchers say, has become the number one leisure activity in Britain, and shopping centres are fast becoming the natural habitat of modern man.

Three American social scientists who studied behaviour in American shopping malls identified four types of shopper. The minimalists dash in and out, neither eating, browsing, nor socialising – shoppers who try to get the whole business over as quickly and inexpensively as possible; traditionalists shop heavily but do little else. Grazers spend ages browsing, eating, and impulse purchasing, while enthusiasts, the most active of all the mall denizens, do it all. The four groups are more or less equal in size. What of those who are 'just looking'? The psychologists have a name for this as well: it's called 'experiential consumption'.

Supermarkets, too, seem to encourage particular behaviour patterns. Let's walk into a typical modern one and see how it works. The chances are that we'll turn right at the door – psychologists say that human beings have a predisposition to turn right on entering closed spaces, even if they are left-handed. That's why most purpose-built supermarkets have their doors on the left.

The first thing to strike the eye will be fresh fruit and vegetables, products that are oddly cheering, even to people who don't eat them. Roughly speaking, products that score as highs will be arranged around the perimeter of a supermarket, with the lows along the aisles. The back wall is an excellent place to sell high-profit items, such as fresh meat, fish, dairy products and delicatessen foods. Position of a product on the shelf is also important: a product at eye-level may sell twice as well as the same product knee-high.

It is easy to assume that the width of the aisles is determined by the size of the trolleys, but they are never too wide – that would encourage people to move too fast and miss opportunities to buy. The ideal is to slow customers down by 'bouncing' them to and fro across the aisle. To accomplish this, the best-selling plain biscuit may be put on one side with the most popular chocolate ones on the other.

Lighting and music can be used to create the right atmosphere. Music is supposed to relax shoppers and slow them down. Lighting is bright at the cosmetics counter to suggest cleanliness, but more subdued in the wine section, where the idea is to convey just a hint of the traditional wine cellar.

---

b 🖉 Find words or phrases in the article with these meanings (the paragraph number is given in brackets).

1 an unpleasant or boring task (1)
2 unreasonable (1)
3 environment (1)
4 looking in a casual way (2)
5 buying something because you see it and like it, not because you really need it (2)
6 inhabitants (2)
7 a tendency towards (3)
8 able to make you feel happy (4)
9 the outside edge (4)
10 long narrow gaps/passages (4)
11 backwards and forwards (5)
12 not bright (6)

3 GRAMMAR Infinitive or -ing form?

a 🖉 Complete these sentences with the correct form of the verbs in brackets.

1 I remember .... that film when it first came out in 1990. (see)
2 First she told us how to get there and then she went on .... where to go and what to do. (recommend)
3 I regret .... my old job; this one's even worse! (leave)
4 Oh no, I've forgotten .... my dental appointment. (cancel)
5 Have you ever tried .... it with yoghurt instead of cream? (make)
6 We regret .... you that flight BA 673 has been delayed. (inform)
7 Did I remember .... the lights? (switch off)
8 She went on .... as though nothing had happened. (eat)
9 I'll never forget .... him play live for the first time. (hear)
10 It was one o'clock so we stopped .... something. (eat)
11 I meant .... you; I saw Paul yesterday. (tell)
12 We can drive there in one day but it'll mean .... very early. (get up)
13 Now that I've got email I've stopped .... to the post office. (go)
14 He went on .... about his problem at work all night long. (talk)

b Choose the correct form of the verb in italics to complete these sentences.

1 Tom's had difficulty *to settle down/ in settling down* in his new school.
2 There's no need *to send/of sending* them a letter; a phone call will do.
3 I have no intention *to apologise/of apologising* to her.
4 He liked the idea *to fly/of flying* by Concorde.
5 His decision *to leave/of leaving* his wife shocked his friends.
6 The thought *to jump/of jumping* out of a plane with only a parachute fills me with horror.
7 I have no wish *to alarm/of alarming* you, but it's the police at the door.
8 Look at the time! We've no hope *to get/of getting* the 8 o'clock train.
9 It's time *to get/for getting* the dinner ready.
10 The company has a plan *to extend/ of extending* its business into the Far East.

4 LISTENING

a You are going to do a dictation. Before you start, write the name of these punctuation symbols.

1 .
2 ,
3 :
4 ;
5 ?
6 !
7 /
8 '
9 "
10 (
11 —

b The dictation is about the English language and whether there is such a thing as a World Standard English. First listen to the whole text without writing anything.

c You are now going to hear the text being dictated, including punctuation. Listen and write what you hear. Then listen to **b** again and check what you have written, paying particular attention to spelling.

5 READING FOR PLEASURE

This story should be read from left to right

The customer is always right, but possibly very stupid. That is the conclusion that the *New Scientist* magazine draws after noticing how companies often state the obvious when labelling everyday products.

The magazine cites as an example of such dumbing-down the warning on a 500g packet of Sainsbury's peanuts – 'Contains nuts'. An American airline was so concerned that passengers might not know what to do with its packets of peanuts that a printed message said: 'Instructions: Open packet, eat contents.'

America is the source of the sillier-seeming alerts. There drivers have stickers on the wing mirrors of bikes and cars saying: 'Remember – objects seen in mirror are behind you.'

Other examples include:

■ From America, an insect spray boasting 'Kills All Insects', but adding: 'Warning – harmful to bees.'

■ From Sweden, a chainsaw whose packaging warns: 'Do not try to stop the chain with hands.'

■ From Britain, a chilled creamy dessert carries the advice 'Do not turn upside down' – on the box bottom. A bread and butter pudding warns: 'Take care – product will be hot after heating.'

And an electrical manufacturer advises: 'Do not iron clothes on body.'

Nytol, a mixture to help people to sleep, cautions that it 'may cause drowsiness'. A cough syrup for young children urges: 'Do not drive car or operate machinery. Avoid alcoholic drinks.'

Translation difficulties may explain advice on a Korean kitchen knife: 'Warning – keep out of children.'

3

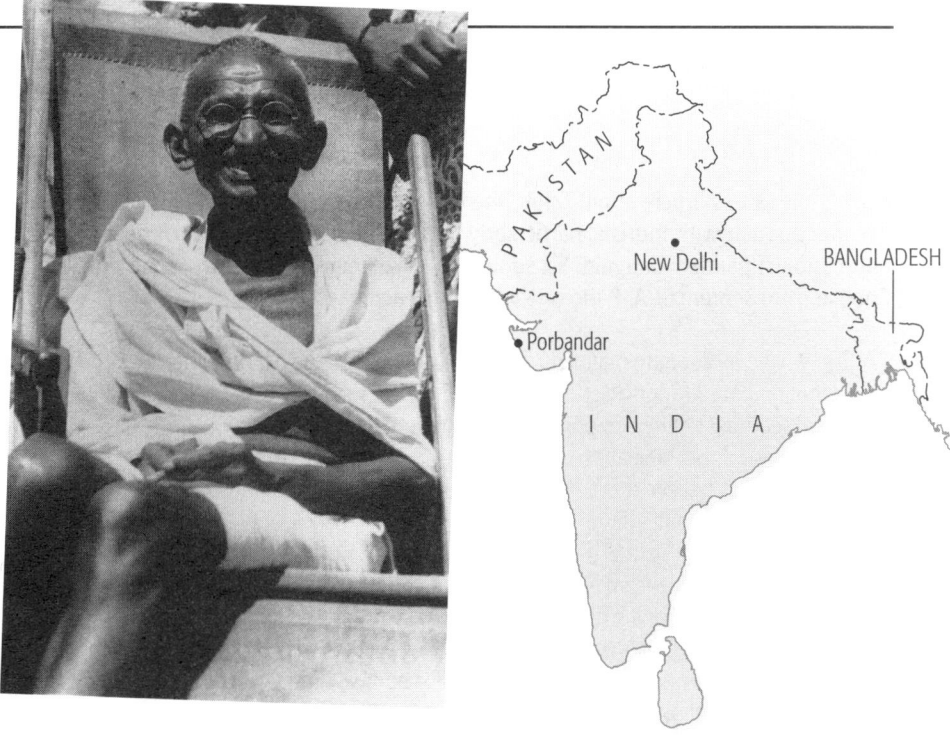

1 LISTENING

🎧 ✍️ You are going to hear a talk about Mahatma Gandhi. He is famous for his work in South Africa, where he spent 21 years trying to obtain more freedom for Indians, and also for his policy of peaceful protest in India to achieve independence. Listen as many times as necessary and complete these notes.

IN BRIEF

Name: _Mahatma Gandhi_

Leader of: 1 ....

○ Mahatma means: 2 ....

Methods and philosophy: 3 ....

FAMILY AND BACKGROUND

Born in Porbandar on: 4 ....

Father's job: 5 ....

Caste: 6 ....

Gandhi means: 7 ....

○ Mother's religion: Jainism; beliefs: 8 ....

As a boy, Gandhi felt guilty about: 9 ....

10 ....

11 ....

12 ....

Age married: 13 ....

○ Studied: 14 .... in: 15 ....

POLITICAL LIFE

Experienced racial discrimination in: 16 ....

January 1915 Gandhi: 17 ....

Massacre of Amritsar turned Gandhi to: 18 ....

Dominant figure in: 19 ....

○ Organised protests against: 20 ....

In prison he went on: 21 ....

Fought for political independence and: 22 ....

Assassinated on: 23 ....

---

2 PRONUNCIATION Linking

In the Coursebook, two types of linking were identified.

Type 1: consonant sound linked to vowel sound, e.g. *it is* /ɪtɪz/.

Type 2: vowel sound + /w/ or /j/ linked to vowel sound, e.g. *do it* /duːwɪt/ and *he is* /hiːjɪz/.

✍️ Look at the introduction to the talk you heard on Gandhi and mark both types of link. Indicate which sound is inserted in the Type 2 links.

Mohandas Karamchand Gandhi, leader of the Indian nationalist movement and known in his later life as Mahatma, which means 'of great soul', was one of the greatest national leaders of the 20th century. His methods and philosophy of non-violent confrontation, or civil disobedience, not only led his own country to independence but influenced political activists of many persuasions throughout the entire world.

3 READING

a 🗝 Read this article about Tahiti, the island in the South Pacific which has become popular with tourists, particularly those interested in the French post-impressionist painter, Gauguin. Six sentences have been removed from the article. Choose from sentences A–F the one which fits each gap (1–6).

A They have a brooding manner: often, in conversation, they shrug and say 'Fiu', denoting boredom or quiet despair – not so much gloomy as reflective.

B I realised how skilfully he portrayed the mysterious listlessness (the 'fiu' mentality) of the Tahitians.

C The Tahitians believe it is a haunted place, fed by an underground river that flows from the spirit world.

D The main town of Fare is a sleepy, unsophisticated huddle of fruit stalls and tiny cafés where people from all over the island come to pass the time of day.

E Bleary-eyed musicians strummed ukuleles as we shuffled, dripping, through Immigration and Customs.

F However, it does not take long to acclimatise and within a few hours I was enjoying the heady atmosphere.

A brush with Gauguin's Nature World

Our flight arrived at Faa'a Airport in Tahiti at five in the morning. As we left the plane the rain pelted down with such force that, by the time we had crossed the tarmac to the terminal, we were soaked. ☐1☐

Then we were presented with garlands of frangipani blossoms and assurances that the rainy season was over, the shower being most unusual for May. Indeed, as soon as the sun rose, the sky cleared, but the air remained clammy and the smell of flowers almost sickly. ☐2☐

The Tahitians are good-looking, in a fleshy, pumped-up way; the men are tall, well proportioned and extravagantly muscled; the women are languid and have soulful eyes. Their language sounds musical but somewhat melancholy, full of sighs and soft-broken vowels. ☐3☐

Although Tahiti is the most-populated island in French Polynesia, it has not lost its beauty. On our way to the Gauguin Museum, we stopped to look at the cave at Mara'a, hidden from the road by a plantation of palms.

The trees gave way to ferns and the grotto appeared like a great semi-circular archway filled with blue-grey water. A trick of the light makes the far wall seem much closer than it is; Gauguin once claimed it took him an hour to swim to the back of the cave. ☐4☐

The Gauguin Museum is spread across a series of pavilions in a botanical garden. It contains few original works but tells the story of the painter's life. ☐5☐

The next stop on our trip was the lush mountainous island of Huahine, about 100 miles northwest of Tahiti. It is much less populated and we felt closer to the real Polynesians. ☐6☐ We were shown a stream heaving with monstrous eels, protected, apparently, by taboo; some lifted their heads from the shallow water and panted like dogs.

b 🗝 Find words in the completed article with these meanings (the paragraph numbers are given in brackets).

1 poured (1)
2 walked without lifting our feet (1)
3 decorative circles of flowers worn around the neck (2)
4 damp and sticky (2)
5 lacking energy, slow-moving (3)
6 deeply expressive (3)
7 plants with long stems and feathery leaves (4)
8 rich in vegetation (6)
9 a number of things close together without order (6)
10 rising and falling (6)

4 GRAMMAR Relative clauses

a 🗝 Look at these pairs of sentences. Which have defining and which have non-defining relative clauses?

1 a People who buy package holidays prefer to relax on holiday.
  b Britons, who traditionally went to the Mediterranean for their holidays, are now travelling further afield.

2 a Backpacking, which usually appeals more to the young, is a cheap way of getting around.
  b What do you think of the campsite we saw yesterday?

3 a That woman that winked at the waiter looks like trouble.
  b The waiter recommended the seafood salad, which was heavenly.

4 a The cash, which I keep in my money-belt, is in dollars.
  b I've already spent the money which I changed at the airport.

b 🗝 Check you have remembered the 'rules' about relative clauses by answering these questions.

1 When can you leave out the relative pronoun?
2 Why do we use commas in non-defining clauses?
3 When can we use *that* instead of *which* or *who*?
4 Does a defining or non-defining clause sound more formal?

c 🔑 In these sentences is the relative pronoun the subject or object of the clause? Write **O** if it is the object or **S** if it is the subject.

1 She brought back the bag that I'd left on the bus. ☐
2 It's the insects that put me off eating outside. ☐
3 He'd read every book that we mentioned. ☐
4 Is that the bus that we're going on the trip in? ☐
5 It was a local taxi driver who told us about this place. ☐
6 Did you get the postcard that I sent? ☐
7 I got a heat rash that wouldn't go away. ☐
8 It's a walk that follows the rim of the crater. ☐
9 She never gave me back the book which she borrowed. ☐
10 I can't find the sunglasses which I left on the table. ☐

d 🔑 Which of the sentences in **c** can be written without the relative pronoun?

5 READING

🔑 Using the wrong expression, or an expression which has a double meaning, can be a cause of great amusement. These notices appeared in hotels and other public places around the world. Read them and try to decide why they are funny.

1 In a Bucharest hotel lobby

> The lift is being fixed for the next day. During that time we regret that you will be unbearable.

2 In a Paris hotel

> *Please leave your values at the front desk.*

3 In a hotel in the former Yugoslavia

> THE FLATTENING OF UNDERWEAR WITH PLEASURE IS THE JOB OF THE CHAMBERMAID.

4 In a Japanese hotel

> You are invited to take advantage of the chambermaid.

5 In the lobby of a Moscow hotel across from a Russian Orthodox monastery

> You are welcome to visit the cemetery where famous Russian and Soviet composers, artists and writers are buried daily except Thursdays.

6 In an Austrian hotel catering for skiers

> Not to perambulate the corridors in the hours of repose in the boots of ascension.

7 In a Bangkok dry cleaners

> DROP YOUR TROUSERS HERE FOR BEST RESULTS.

8 Outside a Paris dress shop

> *Dresses for street walking.*

9 In a Rhodes tailor shop

> Order your summer suit. Because of the big rush we will execute the customers in strict rotation.

10 In a Vienna hotel

> IN CASE OF FIRE, DO YOUR UTMOST TO ALARM THE PORTER.

11 Advertisement for donkey rides in Thailand

> Would you like to ride on your own ass?

12 In a Copenhagen airline ticket office

> *We take your bags and send them in all directions.*

13 In a Norwegian cocktail lounge

> LADIES ARE REQUESTED NOT TO HAVE CHILDREN IN THE BAR.

14 In an Acapulco hotel

> The manager has personally passed all the water served here.

6 READING FOR PLEASURE

SWIM RIGHT UP TO ME
by Katherine Pierpoint

I first learnt to swim at
home in my father's study
On the piano-stool, planted
on the middle of the rug.
Stomach down, head up,
arms and legs rowing hard;
I swam bravely, ploughing
up the small room,
Pinned on a crushed
stuckness of stomach to
tapestry,
The twin handles hard on my
elbows on the back-stroke.
A view down through four
braced wooden legs
To the same thin spot in
the rug.
My mother faced me, calling
rhythmic encouragement,
Almost stepping back to let
me swim up to her,
Reminding me to breathe;
And wiping my hair and eyes
with her hand
As I swam and swam on the
furniture against a running
tide,
Pig-cheeked, concentrating
on pushing and pushing
away,
Planning to learn to fly
next, easy,
Higher than the kitchen
table, even. The garden wall.

9

4

1 VOCABULARY Two-part phrasal verbs

a 🗝 Read this letter, written in the year 2020 by an elderly man to his son, Mike. As you read, underline the phrasal verbs and work out their meaning from the context.

Dear Mike,

Thanks for coming to see me off at the airport; not many people do that nowadays as we all have video wallets. But it was really useful especially when I ran into a few snags with my security documents. I had another problem when I got to London as there was no transport module to pick me up. I had to wait about 20 minutes before one turned up. But anyway, it's great to be here in London with Kate and little Luke and Nancy. They're all going off next month to Australia to visit their cousins. I'm so glad our family hasn't given up visiting each other. I know a lot of people think me old-fashioned but I think we've lost a lot by giving up some of the 'old ways'. I even try to get Luke and Nancy to write but they complain it brings on writer's cramp! And I must admit my back starts playing up when I sit at a desk for any length of time too. Still I am getting on; I'm nearly 110 now.

I can't get over how easily Luke and Nancy use all these complicated technological gadgets they've got in their house. I try not to let on that it's all a bit beyond me sometimes. I think young people have to take on a lot at school these days too – high-level science and communications ... and the speed of everything! Still they seem to pack it all in but studying takes up about 10 hours a day so I suppose it's a good thing they do it all at home with the computer. But I think it's a pity not to have personal contact with classmates and teachers. It turns out that Luke wants to be a historian so he loves asking me questions about the 'old days'. When I got to London the first thing he asked me to do was look at his Museums' CD with him. It was great fun.

Anyway, I just wanted to drop you a line to let you know everything and everybody is fine. Give us a call on the video phone as soon as you have a moment.

Love from everyone

Dad

b 🗝 Match these phrasal verbs (1–5) with the nouns (a–e) they go with.

1 break into   a appearances
2 get through   b a funny smell
3 give off   c a house
4 keep up   d an appointment
5 put back   e a difficult time

c 🗝 Match these nouns (1–5) with the phrasal verbs (a–e) they go with.

1 plans   a drop off
2 effects   b play up
3 a computer   c fall through
4 a problem   d wear off
5 attendance   e come up

d 🗝 Which of the phrasal verbs in **b** and **c** are verbs + prepositions and which are verbs + adverb particles?

e 🗝 Divide these words into three groups – words which are prepositions, words which are adverb particles, and words which are both prepositions and adverb particles when they are used in phrasal verbs. Use a good English–English dictionary to help you.

about across after ahead (a)round aside at away by down for forward from in near out outside over to without

f 🗝 Complete these sentences using words from **e**. You will need to use one word twice.

1 I couldn't do .... my new robot.
2 We couldn't see what he was getting ....
3 It did not take long for him to come .... to the idea.
4 We decided to go .... and book the holiday.
5 She ran .... the hill into the valley.
6 Sit .... immediately!

2 LISTENING

a 🎧 ✎ You are going to hear part of a radio programme called 'Mood Food' about how the food we eat can make us feel good or bad. Before you listen, think about which of these foods put you in a good mood and which put you in a bad mood. Then listen and, according to what you hear, put a tick (✓) for 'feel-good friends' and a cross (✗) for 'feel-good enemies'.

1 caffeine ☐
2 sugary snacks ☐
3 alcohol ☐
4 fruit ☐
5 vegetables ☐
6 seafood ☐
7 soya ☐
8 chicken ☐
9 seaweed ☐

b 🎧 ✎ Listen again and, according to what you hear, choose a verb from the list and complete these sentences.

could   may (× 2)   might
tend to be   can   is likely to   will

1 Caffeine ....
2 A sugary snack ....
3 Alcohol ....
4 Damage to the brain tissue ....
5 People who eat a lot of fruit and vegetables ....
6 Seafood ....
7 Bananas ....
8 Pollution ....

3 GRAMMAR Future forms

✎ Put the verbs in brackets in the most likely future form to complete these sentences. There is sometimes more than one correct answer.

1   When I get a computer, I (can) produce professional-looking work.
2   When I go to college, I (must) find somewhere to live.
3   Do you think you (finished) work by 6pm?
4   The train (leave) at 8 o'clock on Saturday.
5   Just imagine! This time next month I (live) in another country.
6   We (paint) the bathroom blue, but Clare thinks it will make it look too cold.
7   You (stay) just the one night, madam?
8   Look at the sky, it (be) a beautiful day, isn't it?
9   We (play) golf this afternoon. Would you like to come?
10 He's allowed 50 minutes to get to the station. Do you think he (get) there in time?
11 We've booked the hotel we wanted. We (stay) at The Grand.
12 I (order) a taxi for you?
13 I (not go), no matter how often you ask me to!
14 The parties to the contract (have) seven days to cancel this agreement.
15 The Prime Minister (speak) to the nation on Wednesday evening.
16 You (go) next door and apologise to the neighbours for disturbing them.
17 No, Miss Spriggs isn't here. It's Friday afternoon, she (take) choir practice.

4 READING FOR PLEASURE

WHAT'S SO GOOD ABOUT BUG GRUB?

Fifty years ago we turned our noses up at scampi, today it is an everyday food. Could the same thing happen with protein-packed termites, locusts and baby alligators?

Drop into any well-stocked supermarket and you'll discover a range of strange and exotic foodstuffs from around the globe. And they could get even stranger ... You may soon be able to choose from such delights as Candied Cockroach, Chocolate Locust and Mealworm Chow Mein.

It's hard to imagine that many Brits will be rushing to fill up their shopping trollies with this stuff, but in many parts of the world these snacks are considered healthy and tasty, along with caterpillars, flies and even wasps. In fact, in almost every continent apart from Europe insects are eaten as a simple matter of course. And it's not just starving people resorting to bugs because they don't have the option of anything more palatable. Roll up to the very popular Fonda Don Chon restaurant in Mexico City, for example, and you'll be offered anything from cakes made from waterfly eggs to clay-baked crickets.

Mexico is a major consumer of insects, and scoffs about 40 per cent of the 500 different bugs consumed worldwide. Thais go for deep-fried locusts, while dried caterpillars are a delicacy in Zimbabwe. And in Japan fried wasps are considered very fine tucker. So why are we Westerners so turned off by bug eating?

Bugs How they measure up in the nutrition stakes

Nutritional content of edible insects and other animals, based on 100g serving

	Energy (Kcal)	Protein (g)	Iron (mg)	Thiamide (mg)	Riboflavin (mg)	Niacin (mg)
Termite	613	46	0.75	0.13	1.15	0.95
Caterpillar	370	28.2	35.5	3.67	1.91	5.2
Weevil	562	6.7	13.1	3.02	2.24	7.8
Beef (lean)	219	27.4	3.5	0.09	0.23	6.0
Fish (boiled)	170	28.5	1.0	0.08	0.11	3.0

Make your own bug family favourite

Chocolate chirpie chip cookies

$2\frac{1}{4}$ cups of flour
1 tsp baking soda
1 tsp salt
1 cup softened butter
$\frac{3}{4}$ cup white sugar
$\frac{3}{4}$ cup brown sugar
1 tsp vanilla essence
2 eggs
12oz chocolate chips
1 cup chopped nuts
$\frac{1}{2}$ cup dry-roasted crickets

Preparations

Preheat the oven to 375F (190C). In a small bowl, combine the flour, baking soda and salt and set aside. In a large bowl, combine the butter, sugar (white and brown) and vanilla and beat until creamy. Beat in the eggs. Gradually add flour mixture and insects and mix well. Stir in the chocolate chips and nuts. Drop onto a greased cooking tray and bake for 8–10 minutes.

Yummy or what?????

5

Test of Units 1–4

1 INFINITIVE OR -*ING* FORM?

Correct these sentences if necessary. Tick any sentence which is already correct.

1. They made us to wait for one hour.
2. He advised us to invest in new software.
3. She persuaded me choosing the most expensive holiday.
4. He wanted that I meet him as soon as possible.
5. John helped her to reach a decision.
6. We are looking forward to hear from you.
7. Would you mind to open the window?
8. Have you considered getting a robot to do your housework?
9. Don't waste time to make copies for all of us.
10. Have you tried cooking it at a lower temperature?
11. I don't remember to see him before, do you?
12. I regret to send that letter; it caused a lot of embarrassment.
13. He saw her drive away at midnight.
14. We'd like learning golf this summer.
15. He stopped having a break after driving non-stop for four hours.

Total 15

2 SHORT AND LONG VOWELS

Listen and circle the words you hear.

1. reason   risen
2. forks   fox
3. pool   pull
4. cat   cart
5. bird   bard
6. slip   sleep
7. but   boot
8. stalk   stock
9. rug   rag
10. sat   seat

Total 10

3 SPELLING AND SOUNDS

a   Which of these words have the same vowel sound?

bird blue board bored bought caught choose cruise door each fur heard her knew lose piece pour saw shoe short talk theme through tree use war

Total 26

b   Delete the silent letter(s) in these words.

1. health
2. doughnut
3. courtesy
4. snowdrop
5. biscuit
6. while
7. rhyme
8. temperature
9. four
10. knowledge

Total 10

4 LINKING

Which linking sound – /j/ or /w/ – is inserted to link the words in these phrases? If you can, write each phrase in phonetics, e.g. *he is* /hiːjɪz/ (see page 60 for phonetic symbols).

1. come to Iceland
2. he arrived
3. we aren't going
4. two and a half
5. blue eyes
6. pass me a biscuit
7. buy all of them
8. I agree
9. true or false
10. hello everybody

Total 20

5 RELATIVE CLAUSES

a When can we leave out the relative pronoun in a sentence? (2 points)

b Is the relative pronoun the subject or object of its clause in these sentences? Write O for object and S for subject.

1 I can't find my keys which I thought I'd left on the table. ☐
2 It was the guide who recommended this walk. ☐
3 It's the cold that puts me off going to Alaska. ☐
4 I've got a headache that won't go away. ☐
5 Did you get the message that I left on your answerphone? ☐
6 It's a book that describes three generations of the same family. ☐
7 She'd got every CD that he'd ever made. ☐
8 Did we ever return the book that we borrowed from Sarah? ☐
9 Is that the plane that we're flying in? ☐
10 She ate the cake that I'd saved for Tom. ☐

Total 12

6 TWO-PART PHRASAL VERBS

Rewrite these sentences using object pronouns.

e.g. *The treasurer is looking after **the money**. The treasurer is looking after **it**.*
*John put on **the shoes**. John put **them** on.*

1 I'm going to pick up my wife from the station at 6pm.
2 We bumped into Lilly in the supermarket.
3 He got over the shock quite quickly.
4 We'll take on the new workers after Easter.
5 She seemed to frown on the idea.
6 I couldn't get the idea across to her that we only wanted to help.
7 We'll have to put off the match.
8 I picked out this puppy because he was so friendly.
9 He really looks like his mother.
10 We'll have to back the sales manager up on this one.

Total 10

7 FUTURE FORMS

Put the verbs in brackets into the most suitable future form (active or passive) to complete these sentences. There is sometimes more than one correct answer.

1 I can see you're busy so I (finish) the photocopying.
2 We (go) to the theatre on Saturday night so I'm afraid we (not see) you at Jack's party. (2 points)
3 I (post) those letters or you (pass) a post box on your way home? (2 points)
4 Good luck with your exams. I'm sure you (do) well.
5 How time flies! We (be) married for seven years in the spring.
6 Roll on next week. We (sit) on the beach in the Caribbean.
7 The President (announce) his new cabinet later today.
8 Let's get nearer the front. It looks as if the band (start) in a minute.
9 You (dine) in the hotel restaurant this evening?
10 The election (be) next year so the government (have to fulfil) their pre-election promises by then. (2 points)
11 You (do) anything special this evening?
12 The insured (submit) all relevant receipts for work carried out.

Total 15

8 ADJECTIVES FOLLOWED BY PREPOSITIONS

Complete these sentences with an appropriate adjective from the list and the correct preposition.

adept   applicable   commensurate   eligible
incompatible   involved   liable   married   qualified
typical

1 Jack has been _____ his wife for 10 years.
2 Her salary was not _____ her skills.
3 I don't think that applicant is _____ this particular job.
4 I'm afraid this software is _____ the other programs we have on our computers.
5 She became _____ politics from quite an early age.
6 We've become _____ filling in our own tax forms.
7 You may be _____ a grant to help you continue your studies.
8 That accent is _____ the south west.
9 This photocopier is _____ paper jams.
10 I don't think that rule is _____ this situation.

Total 10

6

1 VOCABULARY Adjective + noun collocations

🔑 Match these adjectives (1–15) and nouns (a–o) to make 15 common collocations. There is sometimes more than one correct answer.

1	scudding	a	peaks
2	driving	b	brook
3	rolling	c	thunder
4	searing	d	lane
5	meandering	e	countryside
6	starry	f	clouds
7	leafy	g	rain
8	shimmering	h	suburbs
9	silvery	i	swell
10	babbling	j	sky
11	rumbling	k	heat
12	heaving	l	river
13	dappled	m	sea
14	jagged	n	shade
15	sprawling	o	moon

JOANNA
TROLLOPE
A SPANISH LOVER

'A HUGELY ENJOYABLE BOOK'
Miranda Seymour, *Sunday Times*

2 READING

a 🔑 Joanna Trollope writes stories about people – their lives and loves and the places they live in. In this extract from one of her books, she describes a house. Read it and answer these questions.

1 Find three admirable features of the Grange in the late-eighteenth century.
2 Did the Victorians improve or spoil the house and how?
3 What will Lizzie and Rob use the garden for?
4 What alterations will they make to the property?
5 Why do they think it is the right house for them?

From A Spanish Lover by Joanna Trollope

The Grange had been one of Langworth's best houses in the late-eighteenth century, with a calm and handsome stone façade and a pedimented porch. It had sat then in appropriate gardens, with a gravel sweep between the front door and the
5 street, and lawns behind it, rolling smoothly away to a walled vegetable garden. Now, fussed about with by the Victorians who had added a warren of leaking rooms to the back, and pressed in upon all sides by the modern urgency for new building, the Grange was like a battered old liner
10 crammed into a very small port. New executive dwellings with pictorial nameplates and fancy stonework filled the vegetable garden, and half the lawns had vanished long ago under a street called Tannery Lane, in memory of the nineteenth-century tannery that, for fifty years, had filled the
15 streets of Langworth with a gagging stench. What was left of the Grange garden was plenty big enough, Lizzie and Rob considered, for cricket, bicycles, camps and fighting. The inside of the house was big enough for anything. Surveying the light and beautifully proportioned original rooms, the
20 sweeping staircase, the Victorian muddle at the back that could be knocked through to make a magnificent kitchen-living room, and visualizing the whole painted terracotta and deep-blue and Chinese-yellow, with polished floors and sharp white paintwork, Robert and Lizzie reckoned that the
25 Grange would set the seal upon their success.

b 🔑 Find words or phrases in the text which mean:

1 with a triangular wood or stone decoration above
2 small stones used for driveways
3 a cramped place with many narrow passages
4 worn and damaged
5 squashed into
6 a place where animal skins are made into leather
7 choking, nearly making you vomit
8 confirm/secure

3 VOCABULARY Descriptive verbs

a Storytelling is made more vivid by describing how someone speaks. Match the two halves of these sentences.

1 'Get out of my office,'	a he cheered.
2 'I told you not to say anything,'	b he bellowed.
3 'You shouldn't eat biscuits before dinner,'	c she chortled.
4 'I've just bought the top of the range model,'	d she begged.
5 'Please let us keep the puppy,'	e she wailed.
6 'That means the rest of the cake is for me,'	f she chided.
7 'We've won the cup, hip hip hooray!'	g he snapped.
8 'I want my mummy,'	h he boasted.
9 'Is that the best you can do?'	i he sneered.

b Using different verbs to describe sounds is another storytelling technique. Choose an appropriate verb from the list to complete these sentences, making sure you use a suitable form.

chime   crackle   drone on   moan   rattle   screech   sizzle   squelch
swish   whimper

1 His voice .... and sent most of us to sleep.
2 The sausages .... in the frying pan.
3 I could hear the church bells .... in the distance.
4 As the wind increased, the windows .... in their frames.
5 A welcoming fire .... in the grate.
6 The injured dog was .... as it ran away.
7 Her long evening dress .... across the ballroom floor.
8 We .... our way through the mud and puddles.
9 The patient was .... in pain.
10 The car .... to a halt.

4 GRAMMAR Past tenses and the present perfect

Put the verbs in brackets into a suitable past or present perfect form to complete these sentences. There is sometimes more than one correct answer.

1 As the sun (set) over the sea, she thought of home.
2 Since he (be) a child, he (love) the sea.
3 As we (never be) to Paris before, it (be) difficult to find our way around.
4 We (feel) exhilarated because we (walk) in the mountains all day.
5 The sun (come out) just as we (descend) into the valley.
6 Things (be) much better since we (move) to the countryside.
7 We (not developed) the films yet.
8 I (not see) Jim for ages and then I (see) him twice last week.
9 I (read) a ghost story when the thunder (begin).
10 We had a lazy Sunday afternoon, I (watch) a video while Rob (read) the paper.
11 The last seats (sell) by the time I (phone) last night.
12 She (offer) two jobs in the last week!
13 Anybody (see) my English literature notes?
14 I'm starving! I (not have) time for breakfast this morning.
15 He (be) on the train for 30 minutes before he realised it (go) in the wrong direction.
16 I'm so tired; I (study) all morning.
17 When I got back home, my son (lie) in bed.
18 This is the first time I (eat) this; it's delicious.
19 When you (leave) your last job?
20 When I (walk) into the old part of the town, I (have) the strangest feeling that I (be) there before. But this (be) my first visit to Brindisi.

5 VOCABULARY Linkers

a Which linking word or phrase is the odd one out in these lists?

1 so   therefore   consequently
  as a result   however
  for that reason
2 although   much as   no sooner
  despite the fact that   while
3 furthermore   in brief   besides
  moreover   again   also
4 still   nevertheless   yet
  first and foremost   all the same
  in any case

b Circle the word or phrase which sounds more formal.

1 in addition   what's more
2 instead   on the contrary
3 so   consequently
4 with reference to   talking of
5 in fact   indeed
6 moreover   besides
7 in the same way   correspondingly
8 in conclusion   overall
9 that is   namely
10 for this reason   hence
11 in spite of that   for all that
12 equally   likewise

6 READING

Read this article about Angela Carter, author of *The Werewolf* story in the Coursebook. Then choose the best answer, A, B, C or D, according to the text, to complete the sentences (1–6) which follow.

Carter's recipe for greatness

Three days after Angela Carter's death in 1992, at the age of only 51, her publisher Virago sold out entirely of her books. There was a certain irony in this. Only a year earlier the judges for the Booker Prize had failed even to put her last novel, Wise Children, on their shortlist, provoking an outcry on the part of many discerning contemporary critics. The minute she was dead, with hardly a decent interval, Carter's distinctive and original writing was widely acclaimed, as it has continued to be ever since. She would have found the macabre tinge to her elevation to celebrity author status amusing – she had a taste for the bizarre, and a sharp-tongued acuteness about insincerity of any kind.

Angela Carter was, critics are now agreed, a novelist of lasting greatness, whose Nights at the Circus and Wise Children have become classics of the genre known as 'magic realism'. Her prose journalism has inspired a generation of young writers. Her books figure prominently on reading lists in most university departments of literature, both in Britain and America. But, as these new and reissued volumes should remind us, she was never solemn, nor self-important. She was consistently funny, both in her fiction and her extensive non-fiction.

I'd never read her early novel Love. It contains all the Carter ingredients: fantasy, curious sex, passion distorted, hopes and fears, and above all the meticulously observed detail of her characters' most intimate lives. The novel coolly observes the two intensely bonded brothers Lee and Buzz, and Lee's girlfriend Annabel, locked into a triangle of erotic fantasy from which they cannot escape. There are some uncomfortable self-conscious moments in the construction of the tale, of a kind which are not to be found in Carter's later writing. But the language already has a mesmerising intensity, designed deliberately to trouble the reader, because the plot is so resolutely inconsequential.

The new volume of her collected works containing her journalism, Shaking a Leg, is packed with deliciously tongue-in-cheek wit about the everyday world of the 1970s and 1980s. She is mistress of the arresting opening and the bathetic ending. The great surprise for me among her collected writings, however, was her radio plays. I must have heard some of them. But to read them is to tap another vein in Carter's rich creativity. She has an extraordinary ear, for language itself and for the minutiae of noise which fills every nook and cranny of our waking and dreaming lives. Vampirella, a variation on the Dracula theme in Carter's inimical dream-mythical style, reads as grippingly as it must have sounded on air. I found her screenplay for The Company of Wolves more interesting than the film itself.

1 Immediately after Angela Carter's death,
   A her publisher did not want to sell her novels.
   B she won a major literary prize.
   C there was a rush on sales of her books.
   D the literary critics turned against her.

2 Angela Carter would have reacted to her change of fortune with
   A pride.
   B amusement.
   C arrogance.
   D bitterness.

3 Angela Carter's novels are read on literature courses because
   A she wrote in many different styles.
   B young people can relate to her.
   C she wrote two epic novels.
   D her work has stood the test of time.

4 A possible weakness of her early writing was that
   A she distanced herself too much from her characters.
   B there was some awkward development of the plot.
   C the plot was too complicated.
   D the language was too self-conscious.

5 The language in her early writing is
   A complex and difficult to understand.
   B intentionally rich in verb tenses.
   C able to hold the reader's attention in a challenging way.
   D easy to remember because it is disturbing.

6 Her radio plays
   A show her awareness of the sound of the language.
   B were never meant to be recorded.
   C would have made better films than radio broadcasts.
   D rely on the skill of the actor for success.

7

1 READING AND WRITING

Read this informal note from a friend. Using the information in the note, complete the formal notice which follows with a maximum of three words per gap. The first one has been done for you.

---

e-mail

Normal

FROM:
TO:
CC:
BCC:

Message

Here's the info I promised you about the next society meeting. Do you think you could make up the notice for it because, as you know, next week I'm away on holiday?

An old friend of mine, Trish Roberton (yes, the famous historian from Edinburgh University!), has said she'll do the talk for the society on 22 June. She's done loads of work on the history of the Highlands and Islands of Scotland so she's going to talk about evidence of 'ancient man', then changes in the weather and geography. She's got lots of slides and some great Celtic music to go with the talk. I've actually managed to get 10 cassettes of the music to sell. As we'll have about 50 people there, I don't think we'll have enough cassettes, but that's all the shop had.

Shall we make the talk 7.30pm as usual? It's a Wednesday I think. I can get Eddie Burns to sell the tickets and of course we can always sell them to people as they go in on the night. Eddie's number is Broadford 372835.

Give me a ring if you've got any problems.

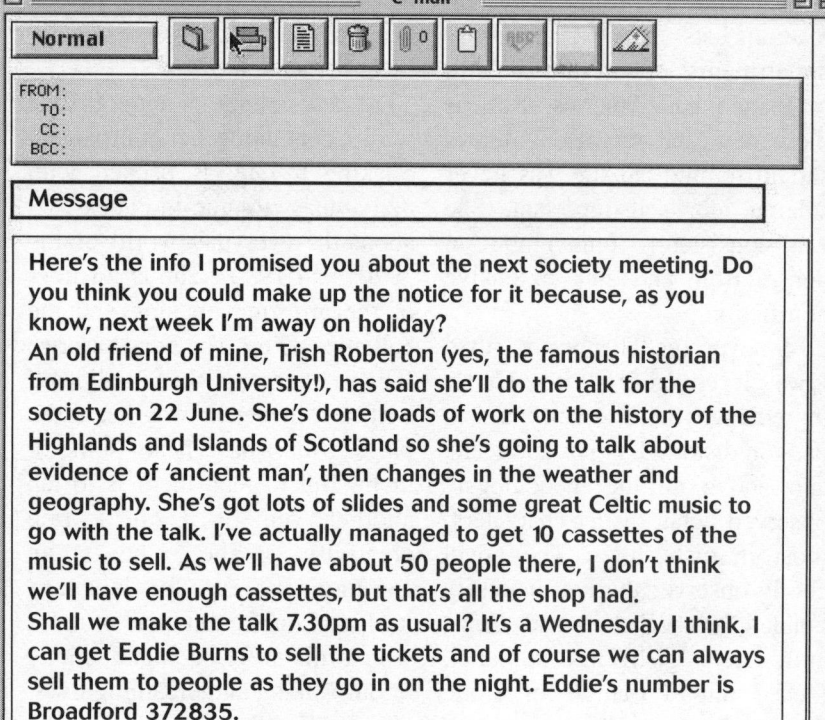

Broadford Historical Society

Lecture and slides – The History of Scotland's Highlands and Islands

Trish Roberton, famous [1] _historian_ from Edinburgh University, [2] .... on the history of Scotland's Highlands and Islands. [3] .... to describing fascinating evidence of [4] .... , she will also explain the [5] .... and [6] .... changes which have taken place. The talk will be [7] .... by slides and traditional Celtic music. Cassettes of the music [8] .... However the number of cassettes is [9] .... The talk will [10] .... at 7.30pm [11] .... 22nd June. Tickets are [12] .... from Eddie Burns [13] .... 372835 or [14] .... door.

2 GRAMMAR
First conditional

a Match the two halves of these sentences.

1 If you eat all that cake,
2 If you are thinking of leaving early again,
3 Unless he's phoned to say otherwise,
4 Unless they've changed the timetable,
5 As long as she's been keeping to her diet plan,
6 Should the President be delayed,
7 Provided we use the new printers,
8 If he makes another sexist remark like that,
9 If it's that awful Mr Kempton,
10 Even if he has it typed up on a memo,

a we're meeting at 4 o'clock.
b shall I say you're in a meeting?
c I won't buy presents for his wife; it's not my job.
d you are going to be sick.
e I'll be handing in my notice.
f I'm going to tell the boss.
g she'll have lost about 5 kilos by now.
h the first train leaves at 5.15 on Saturday.
i these photos are going to look stunning.
j lunch is to be postponed.

b Complete these sentences with a suitable ending. The first two have been done for you.

1 If you don't need English for this job, _why are you studying it?_

2 If you are in pain, _go to the doctor's._

3 If you are hot,

4 Should symptoms persist,

5 If it's a better job,

6 If you're putting on weight,

7 If you like Mexican food,

8 If you like her,

3 LISTENING

a 🔈 You are going to hear a dialogue between two young men. They are talking about a television programme they saw last night. They are friends and they are using very informal language. Before you listen, match these colloquial words and expressions (1–5) to their more neutral equivalents (a–e).

1	bloke	a	become angry
2	the box	b	man
3	banger	c	children
4	mint	d	TV
5	kids	e	car
6	throw a wobbly	f	fortune

b 🔈🔈 Listen and, according to what you hear, decide whether these sentences about the man featured on TV and his wife are true or false. Write T for true and F for false.

1   The man on TV was well dressed. ☐
2   He lives in a luxurious flat in town. ☐
3   The old cars he drives are valuable. ☐
4   His two sons are following in his footsteps. ☐
5   His wife looks like a million dollars. ☐
6   His wife is rich in her own right. ☐
7   He doesn't want to have electricity in his house. ☐
8   His wife is likely to go along with his latest idea. ☐
9   He isn't interested in keeping his wealth. ☐

c 🔈🔈 Listen again and try to work out the meanings of these informal words and phrases from the context.

1   going on about
2   specs
3   he reckons
4   is rubbish
5   straight up
6   off his head
7   mod cons
8   they're a right pair
9   missus (comes from the title Mrs)
10 she's worth a bob or two
11 to keep him on the straight and narrow
12 a lost cause
13 whatsisname
14 trendy
15 a tenner
16 I bet
17 take him to the cleaners

WARNING Unless you are an extremely fluent speaker of a language, it might be better to avoid using very colloquial language as it can sound extremely strange when used by the wrong person in the wrong place at the wrong time!!!

4 READING

🔈 Read the article on page 20 about burglaries at English stately homes. Then choose the best answer, A, B, C or D, according to the text, to complete these sentences.

1   At Ripley Castle, someone should have suspected the burglar because
    A   he was accompanied by a strange-looking woman.
    B   he asked if he could follow on his own.
    C   he said he was a military man.
    D   he knew little about historic houses.

2   It is believed Earl and Lady Dudley were robbed because
    A   they live in a very wealthy part of London.
    B   Lady Dudley had bought a diamond ring eight days before.
    C   they had recently appeared in a glossy magazine.
    D   they are part of the National Stately Homes Hotline.

3   Nowadays thieves want to steal
    A   specific valuable objects.
    B   televisions and videos.
    C   small, easily concealed items.
    D   attractive garden ornaments.

4   The modern thief is
    A   more determined.
    B   more experienced.
    C   more believable.
    D   better informed.

5   Rich people could be said to be responsible themselves because
    A   they all live in the same part of London.
    B   they walk in the streets in London.
    C   they have poor security in their homes.
    D   they 'advertise' their possessions.

6   The rich agree to appear in magazines because
    A   they are often looking for a new husband or wife.
    B   they need money.
    C   they adore being famous.
    D   they are proud of their ancestry.

7   The illegal trade in stolen arts and antiques
    A   is a type of white-collar crime.
    B   is a favourite of the drug barons.
    C   is becoming more of an international problem.
    D   ranks third in estimated value.

8   Philip Saunders warns that potential thieves might visit a stately home
    A   after going through a glossy magazine.
    B   pretending to be fishermen.
    C   to get information about security devices.
    D   on a tip-off from some other villains.

Rich pickings

When the Earl and Countess of Dudley invited Hello! magazine into their home, they may also have opened their doors to burglars, who use the glossies to find their next stately target.

He looked every inch a military man, even down to the lingering war wound that made him limp so badly. At Ripley Castle in north Yorkshire, on a wet May bank holiday afternoon, nobody suspected that the elderly gentleman was anything but an avid admirer of Britain's historic homes. Yet when he left the castle, still stiff-gaited, he was not empty-handed. There was a priceless Civil War sword, once carried by an officer in the 1644 Battle of Marston Moor, pushed down his trouser leg. His female accomplice had a fur and leather coat, worn in the same skirmish, rolled up beneath her anorak. The couple escaped scott-free.

That was the day that Sir Thomas Ingilby, the 41-year-old owner of Ripley, decided to set up the National Stately Homes Hotline to combat crime against the aristocracy who open their houses and grounds to the public. 'The sword was carried into battle by an Ingilby ancestor,' he said last week. 'It was taken off the wall by this 60-year-old man who told our guide that because of his gammy leg he would wait at the top of the castle and follow the other visitors down slowly. That's when he seized it and put it down his trousers. It transpired that he and the woman had robbed four other historic homes over the previous three weeks.'

Ingilby, whose father first let in visitors in 1954, had fallen victim to a very modern crime: theft from the rich and famous, whose addresses, and valuable possessions, are often detailed in magazine articles, on television programmes, and in reference books. Only last week, the Earl of Dudley and his wife, the former actress Maureen Swanson, were robbed at knife-point by two intruders who stole jewellery worth thousands of pounds from their London house.

Just eight days before, the Dudleys had posed in photographs at their home – Lady Dudley sporting a rare diamond ring – for Hello! magazine.

Could it be the so-called curse of Hello!? Appearing in glossy magazines' welcoming pages, so they say, used to mean you were likely to lose your spouse. Now it looks as if your possessions are up for grabs as well.

'If you go back a few years, it was the television and video that thieves went for. They could flog those around the corner for £30,' says Colin Reeve, director of security at Christie's auction house in London. 'But now, with antiques programmes on television, magazines showing lovely homes, and the publicity attached to every sale of art work, the thief knows exactly what the value is. The thief is much more knowledgeable these days. I have known a five-ton fountain disappear from the middle of a lake at a country house before now. The size and weight of a piece does not deter today's burglar; he's very sophisticated indeed.'

Too true, agrees Detective Chief Inspector Charles Hill, head of the CID in Belgravia, London, who ran Scotland Yard's art and antiques squad until quite recently. He says that the rich who live in his patch, the most valuable few square miles of the capital, have become careless.

'Well-coiffured women wander along the street to Harrods wearing Rolex watches worth £3,000 on their wrists, and wonder why they get robbed. If you drape yourself over the sofa with all your possessions around you in a magazine article, it is lighting a fireball in the night. It obviously alerts burglars, and these people have only themselves to blame for what follows.'

We live in changing times. The aristocracy – and the just plain rich – no longer exist apart from the common herd. They often appear in various forms to promote their ancestral piles, which are open to the public in order to pay tax bills and roof repairs. An article in a glossy magazine, jokily known as the Burglars' Bible, will not be sniffed at.

Interpol has calculated that the illegal trade in arts and antiques is now third only to drugs and white-collar crime, with worldwide illicit sales between £3 billion and £10 billion each year. Works of art are often stolen to order. A Titian painting, worth an estimated £5m, vanished from a stately home recently. It is now on the art world's most-wanted list. But it may have been an easy picking for the house is open to the public all year round. Detectives believe that the thieves, who climbed a ladder before smashing a window into the drawing room, must have made reconnaissance visits as ordinary ticket-paying visitors. Several lights in the garden were covered up during the raid.

Philip Saunders, the editor of Trace, a magazine established to retrieve stolen arts and antiques, advises the official guides at ancestral homes on how to spot the bad apples among their visitors. 'There was one chap going round a castle who kept bending down and tying up his shoelaces,' he recalls. 'It turned out that this man was wearing socks with prominent stripes at regular intervals. He was using them to precisely measure how high the infrared security rays were fixed above the floor. Another fellow was spotted walking around a house with a fisherman's walking stick, marked rather like a ruler. He was up to the same thing. One respectable-looking gentleman was discovered by police visiting historic homes to make floor plans to sell to villains.'

8

1 READING AND WRITING

a Choose three colours which you feel strongly about and write about 100 words describing them and their associations for you. Do not spend too much time thinking – look at the colour chart in the Coursebook and write spontaneously!

Black   Grey   White

b Look at what you have written, in particular the way you have written *th*, and read the interpretation of your handwriting on the right.

c What do you think of the interpretation? To what extent do you think a person's handwriting can reveal their character?

2 VOCABULARY
Word-building

Write the nouns from these adjectives.

1 ambitious
2 sympathetic
3 gentle
4 dextrous
5 benevolent
6 lonely
7 delicate
8 modest
9 idealistic
10 innovative

Your handwriting and you

Partnerships

The letters t and h together tell us how a person treats his or her partner. In order to make the 'th' coupling work, you have to imagine that the writer's feelings and behaviour are embodied in the t while the partner's reaction is portrayed by the h standing alongside him.

If all is going well and the relationship is balanced and flourishing, then the two letters will complement each other, standing side by side, touching gently. They will not be separated nor intertwined to the point of suffocation.

If the cross-bar slashes right across the t until it overhangs the hoop of the h, it means the writer craves dominance over their partner and will tend to be an overbearing presence in the partnership.

If the t cross-bar reaches out wildly, dragging the h towards it, you have the scenario of the one very demanding partner using the full force of their emotions to compel the other to succumb to his or her wishes. Emotional blackmail may be involved, or it could simply be a battle of wills, one which the writer is currently winning. Whatever lies at the root of it, this is a volatile relationship packed with imbalance.

When a t foists itself upon an h and when the h, in its turn, seems to be trying to escape and run away, it is telling you that the partner is desperate to break away. Unconsciously we know when our partners are unhappy, yet so often we choose to acknowledge the problem only when it is much too late.

Other th's to look out for:

Cross-bar slices high across the stem. The writer is not the emotional type. Being rational in their approach to relationships, they will discuss bonding, passion and romance without really understanding them.

 t and h connected by a hoop. The writer uses a fierce intellect to impose ideas and plans on their partner. If the partner likes such things, fine. If not, it could lead to ructions.

 Severely disconnected cross-bar flies over h. The writer is divorced from their true feelings and has problems expressing affection and is afraid this may drive their partner away. So they keep a firm grip, hanging on, maintaining control, always ensuring that their partner never wanders off.

3 GRAMMAR Conditional forms

a Which of these sentences are facts and which are suppositions?

1 If you want to join the club, it costs £500 for the year.
2 If she had time, I'm sure she would help me with my homework.
3 If she had time, she helped me with my homework.
4 If he hadn't finished his work, he brought it home with him.
5 If he hadn't gone to the party, he would never have met her.

b Put the verbs in brackets in the most suitable conditional form to complete these sentences. There is sometimes more than one correct answer.

1 If you (go) to university in the United States next year, you (live) on campus?
2 I (write) a letter of complaint right now if I (be) you.
3 I (pick up) you at 3pm tomorrow if you (wait) on the corner.
4 If you (have) dinner now, I (call back) later.
5 If you (like) to take a seat, I (tell) Mr Johnson you are here.
6 I think if you (use) more colour in the painting now, it (look) too busy.
7 If there (not be) a postal strike last week, we (get) the information on time.
8 He (win) that last game if he (not lose) his concentration.
9 We (be) happier if we (live) by the sea, I think.
10 If she (get) better qualifications when she was younger, she (not be) in such a dead-end job now.
11 It (be) all right if I (come) a bit later?
12 We (appreciate) it if you (confirm) your place by next Monday.
13 If she (leave) two hours ago, she (arrive) at the hotel by now.
14 If only I (take) traveller's cheques, I (not lose) so much money.
15 If you (want) that new job, you (have to) brush up on your languages.

4 VOCABULARY Prefixes

a Complete this article about modern city life using words from the list with a suitable prefix added. The first one has been done for you.

cultures   dogs   enemies   grown   lingual   political   social   husbands

URBAN CULTURE

The growth and internationalisation of city life in the twentieth century has given rise to a new urban culture, characterised by numerous ¹...*subcultures*... , all expressing their ideas through art and music. Any idea of a monoculture has long since been ²............. – variety and diversity are today's buzzwords.

³............. city culture enriches life with diverse literature, lyrics and poetry, but it can also breed highly political creatures, who succeed at the expense of society's ⁴............. . In the face of such injustices it is hard for anyone to remain ⁵............. . Or is it? Do today's city dwellers simply ignore the most crass of ⁶............. behaviour as they hurry by?

Some argue that relationships have become commodities. ⁷............. or wives can be easily discarded as they are absorbed into the anonymity of the city. This was not the case in yesterday's small towns and villages, where they would more likely than not become ⁸............. , forced into painful close contact on a daily basis.

b Match these prefixes (1–10) with the words they can go with (a–j). There is sometimes more than one correct answer.

1	anti	a	active
2	co	b	social
3	de	c	classical
4	fore	d	runner
5	hyper	e	form
6	inter	f	scientific
7	neo	g	exist
8	over	h	locking
9	pseudo	i	arm
10	trans	j	forestation

5 PRONUNCIATION /s/ and /ʃ/ + /ʃ/ and /tʃ/

a  Listen and number the words you hear.

SHE	SEE	SHIP	CHIP
SHELF	SELF	SHOES	CHOOSE
CHIN	SHIN	ASS	ASH
WHICH	WISH	CHEAP	SHEEP
SHEET	SEAT	SHARE	CHAIR
MASH	MASS	CASH	CATCH

b Join the words you have numbered together. Which letter of the alphabet does it make?

6 LISTENING FOR PLEASURE

Colours
by Yevtushenko

When your face
appeared over my crumpled life
at first I understood
only the poverty of what I have.
Then its particular light
on the woods, on rivers, on the sea,
became my beginning in the coloured world
in which I had not yet had my beginning.
I am so frightened, I am so frightened,
of the unexpected sunrise finishing,
of revelations
and tears and the excitement finishing.
I don't fight it, my love is this fear,
I nourish it who can nourish nothing,
love's slipshod watchman.
Fear hems me in.
I am conscious that these minutes are short
and that the colours in my eyes will vanish
when your face sets.

About the author

Yevtushenko was born in 1933, in Zima, Russia. He moved to Moscow in 1944, where he studied at the Gorky Institute of Literature. His early poetry, such as *The Third Snow* (1955), made him a spokesperson for the young post-Stalin generation. In 1960 he began to travel abroad to give readings of his poetry. His first major stage piece, *Under the Skin of the Statue of Liberty*, was a huge success in 1972. He has also written a novel and other prose works and engaged in acting and photography.

1 READING

a 🖋 Read this article about four girls who play American football. Six paragraphs have been removed from the article. Choose from paragraphs A–F the one which fits each gap (1–6).

Latino girls shake up the field

LA quartet make history as they invade the male stronghold

The success of the United States women's soccer team who won the World Cup in Pasadena has further
5 established the game among girls in America. Now a group of high school students are hoping to have an impact, albeit
10 more modest, on the real bastion of male sport in the country: American football.

1

If girls had a role to play it was as cheerleaders or, if
15 they were lucky, taking part in an annual game of what was called 'powderpuff football' in which they were allowed to perform at high
20 school in a game against one another. Now, thanks to a quartet of young Latino women at Lincoln

high school in Los Angeles,
25 things are changing.

2

Their arrival on the team has created a major stir both in Los Angeles and nationally. In LA the game needed a
30 happier story to tell in the wake of two highly publicised court cases involving football stars who had illegally used disabled
35 parking stickers. The city is also currently without its own professional team, although it is involved in a bid for a franchise in
40 competition with Houston to bring the game back here.

3

'I wanted to do something new,' said Cruz when asked why she

45 chose such a demanding sport. Football proved more challenging than basketball or soccer.

4

Leo Castro, the team
50 coach, said that he has been impressed with the girls' resolution and fearlessness: 'They tell the guys that they want to be
55 hit hard.' He said they set a good example to the male members of the team.

5

Whether others will be tempted to follow their
60 example may depend on how well they do this season, which started with a 42–6 defeat by the Roosevelt high school team.

6

A For the first time four girls are lining up for the Lincoln Tigers in the high school football season. Two of them, Diocelina Macias and Luisana Cruz, are running backs and two, Imelda Chaparro and Patricia Mora, are linemen or, as some commentators are calling them, linewomen.

B At present, women and girls make up a remarkable 41 per cent of soccer players in the US and, among girls in the 6–11 age group, soccer is now second only to basketball. The pioneers in the Lincoln Tigers colours know they have a long, long climb ahead of them if American football is ever to attract anything like that sort of interest from their sisters.

C The male team members at the school, which is in a predominantly Latino area of east LA, have been largely supportive. 'I really respect them for getting out there and sticking with it,' the linebacker Roger

Sepulveda told the Los Angeles Times. 'They don't quit, they keep coming back for more.'

D Few games in the world seem more geared towards male exclusivity, with a high premium placed on beef and muscle. Boys under a certain height and weight have long realised that their sporting future was more likely to lie on the baseball field, the tennis court or the golf course.

E The girls have already been courted by the talk shows, have appeared on Women 2 Women, the CBS all-women news show, and draw photographers and reporters when they hit the field.

F Chaparro said of the boys they play against: 'You're waiting for them to come and hit you but you get a rush out in the field and you really don't feel it.' The girls wear the traditional protective gear plus some additional chest padding.

b 🖋 Read through the article again and answer these questions (the information in brackets tells you where in the article to look).

1 Find a word which means even if it is. (lines 1–12)
2 Which word echoes the word *stronghold* in the subtitle? (lines 1–12)
3 What do *cheerleaders* do and why? (line 14)
4 What do you think is implied in the phrase '*powderpuff football*'? (lines 17–18)
5 Explain the phrase *created a major stir*. (line 27)
6 Find a phrase which means following a first event. (lines 26–41)
7 What are synonyms for *resolution* and *fearlessness*? (lines 52–53)
8 Find a word which means people who give a description of an event which is broadcast. (paragraph A)
9 What does the phrasal verb *make up* mean in this context and what other four meanings does the verb have? (paragraph B)
10 Why does the journalist use the word *climb*? (paragraph B)
11 Find a phrase which means organised for that purpose. (paragraph D)
12 Explain the phrase *with a high premium placed on beef and muscle*. (paragraph D)
13 What does the phrase *courted by the talk shows* mean? (paragraph E)
14 Why do you think the news show is called *Women 2 Women*? (paragraph E)
15 Find a word which means attract. (paragraph E)
16 Explain the phrase *get a rush*. (paragraph F)
17 What does the word *gear* mean in this context and what other meaning does it have? (paragraph F)

2 GRAMMAR *wish, if only, would rather, it's time*

✎ **Finish rewriting these sentences so they have the same meaning as the original. The first one has been done for you.**

1 The company hasn't put on a new production for years.
I wish *the company would put on a new production* .

2 The percussionist is always falling asleep during the performance.
If only ....

3 I would like to sit next to the keyboard players, not the string section.
I'd rather ....

4 I didn't study classical music at college.
I wish ....

5 Mr Wilson doesn't want to play in a modern musical.
Mr Wilson would rather ....

6 Claudette lost her music on the underground.
Claudette wishes ....

7 This stage is too small.
It's time ....

8 I haven't enough money to buy a new violin.
If only ....

9 I don't want Kate to take that job in Manchester.
I'd rather ....

10 We think Eric should retire; he's 73.
It's time ....

11 I'm sorry Fiona has to leave the company.
I wish ....

12 It's 11.30pm. Home time!
It's time ....

13 I'd like my husband to be rich and famous.
If only ....

14 I just can't remember the name of the theatre.
I wish ....

3 VOCABULARY Prefixes and suffixes

a ✎ **Choose the correct adjective in italics to complete these sentences. In two sentences both alternatives are correct.**

1 The kitchen was *unusable/useless* as it had no mains water connected.
2 Much to the owner's horror, the fire destroyed a *worthless/priceless* medieval musical instrument.
3 I bought a smaller car because it is more *economic/economical*.
4 The signing of the Peace Treaty today is of *historical/historic* importance.
5 He asked a lot of questions but was *unsatisfied/dissatisfied* with the answers.
6 *Exhausting/exhaustive* preparation for the show paid off.
7 Destruction of the environment is an *emotional/emotive* issue.

b ✎ **What is the difference in meaning between the pairs of adjectives in a? If possible, use a good English–English dictionary to help you.**

4 LISTENING

🎧 ✎ **You are going to hear a disc jockey talking on the radio about night clubs in Europe. Listen and, according to what you hear, decide whether these statements are true or false. Write T for true and F for false.**

1 In northern Europe the music must be played through good equipment. ☐
2 In Britain people love a club to be crowded. ☐
3 The appearance of a club is not so important in Italy. ☐
4 A club in Amsterdam is a masterpiece of design. ☐
5 Southern Europeans show their feelings. ☐
6 People in industrialised areas prefer 'house' music. ☐
7 The music in Britain reflects the calm lifestyle. ☐
8 Germany has really good DJs. ☐
9 Berlin has a long techno music tradition. ☐
10 Frankfurt has more amazing clubs than other German cities. ☐

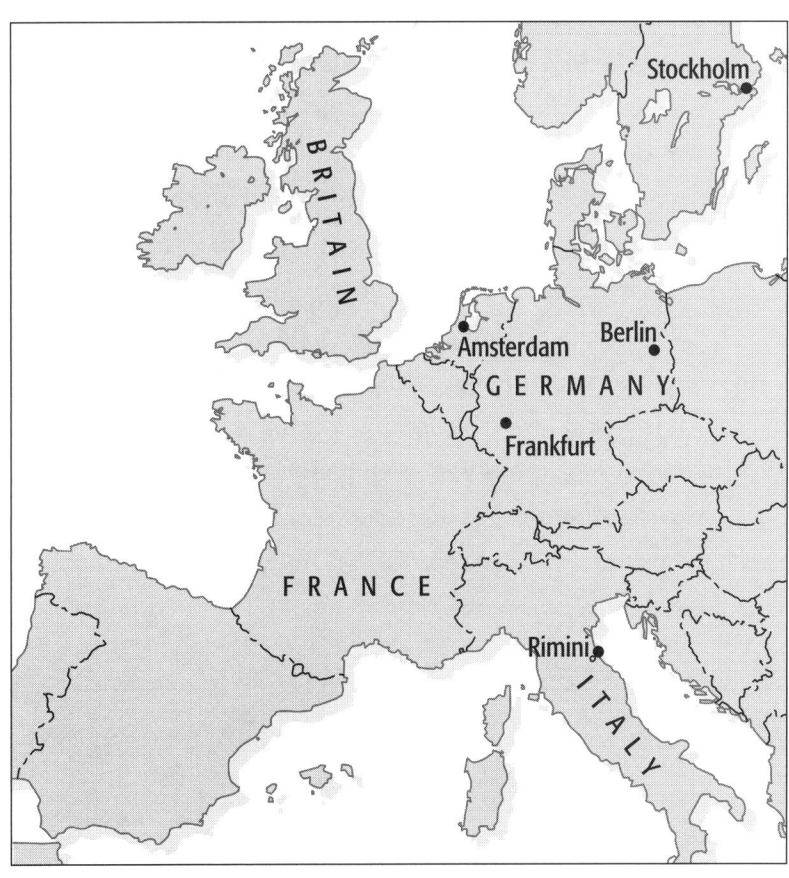

5 VOCABULARY Adjective + noun collocations

Match these adjectives (1–10) with the most likely nouns (a–j) to make 10 adjective + noun collocations which you might find in a film review. Sometimes more than one answer is possible. Use an English–English dictionary or dictionary of collocations to help you.

1	hair-raising	a	slot
2	unexpected	b	set
3	gripping	c	villain
4	stunning	d	car chase
5	fetching	e	entertainment
6	bloodthirsty	f	screenplay
7	original	g	plot
8	solid	h	thriller
9	contrived	i	twist
10	two-hour	j	actress

6 READING AND EDITING

Some people take up very demanding hobbies which become a way of life. This newspaper article is about Tracy Edwards, a yachtswoman who set herself a real challenge!

Read the text carefully. In most lines there is one unnecessary word. Write the word at the end of the line. If a line is correct, put a tick against the line number. Two lines have been done for you.

7 PRONUNCIATION
Consonant clusters

a What are these words? Write them down.

1	/præktɪs/	6	/friːkwənt/
2	/θæŋkt/	7	/kwɪkliː/
3	/skuːl/	8	/ənaʊnst/
4	/fɪfθs/	9	/dredfʊl/
5	/swɒləʊ/	10	/mɑːtʃt/

b Listen and repeat the words in **a**.

c Write these words in phonetics.

1	flames	6	crash
2	speak	7	helped
3	twenty	8	sixths
4	punched	9	grated
5	tasks	10	scratch

d Listen and repeat the words in **c**.

International yachtswoman Tracy Edwards's racing catamaran was yesterday	1 .....✓.....
expected to set forth a new transatlantic record for a vessel crewed entirely by women.	2 ..forth..
The transatlantic crossing is the first of three voyages by the 10 women.	3 ....
During her latest voyage, Tracy described about the hardships she and her	4 ....
crew were facing, on the same waters which had been claimed the *Titanic*.	5 ....
She said on a ship-to-shore call: 'The weather is also pretty horrendous.	6 ....
It is five degrees below freezing with the wind right on the nose, making the	7 ....
boat toss all around or shudder through the waves. Just when you think	8 ....
you have got your balance, the boat it pitches. We have a few bumps and	9 ....
bruises and several of us are feeling pretty queasy.	10 ....
'Everyone is so drenched to the skin and having to sleep fully clothed, so that	11 ....
they can be ready to deal with icebergs. When you see them so on the	12 ....
radar it is worse than to seeing them for real, because as you hurtle	13 ....
through the blackness your own imagination works overtime.'	14 ....
However, despite of the discomfort, Tracy said her international crew had	15 ....
been 'fantastic'. She added, 'All that matters is the weather, the sea and	16 ....
what you are doing at the time.'	17 ....

10 Test of Units 6–9

1 PAST TENSES AND THE PRESENT PERFECT

Put the verbs in brackets into an appropriate form (present perfect simple/continuous, past simple/continuous, past perfect simple/continuous) to complete these sentences. There is sometimes more than one correct answer.

1 Since Leila (be) three years old, she (play) the violin. (2 points)
2 The actors (feel) bored because they (play) the same parts for years. (2 points)
3 Things (be) much better for the actors once they (move) into the new theatre. (2 points)
4 I (not be) to the cinema for ages and then I (see) two films last week. (2 points)
5 The last tickets (sell) by the time we (get) to the theatre. (2 points)
6 Sean Bean (make) two films in the last year.
7 I (talk) to that woman for half an hour before I (realise) who she was. (2 points)
8 This is the first time I (be) to the ballet. It's beautiful.
9 As the band (play), someone in the audience (jump) onto the stage. (2 points)
10 The lights (go out) just as we (try) to find our seats. (2 points)
11 We (not see) his latest film yet.
12 Anybody (see) my copy of *Time Out*?

Total 20

2 LINKERS

Correct the linkers in these sentences if necessary. Tick any sentence which is already correct.

1 Besides her aunt was ill, Mary took her some flowers.
2 Although he was alone in the house, he wasn't frightened.
3 Because her kind nature, Elizabeth offered to look after her neighbour.
4 It was so a fright when I saw the blood that I ran out of the room.
5 He studied Spanish yet he could travel round South America.
6 With regard to your application, we are pleased to inform you that you have been accepted for the post.
7 For conclusion, I would just like to thank you all for being here today.
8 Despite of writing to her many times, he never got a reply.
9 She was charming, yet Brian couldn't help feeling suspicious of her motives.
10 We had such little time to catch the train, we had to miss the last act of the play.

Total 10

3 READING AND EDITING

Some lines in this article have an extra word. Write the word at the end of the line. If the line is correct, put a tick against the line number. Two lines have been done for you.

Total 14

All light on the night
Bright lights could help nightshift workers to overcome tiredness

Our cities and towns are far from silent at the night. As most of us are   1 ....the....
going to bed, a battalion of workers is just stirring into action.   2 ....✓......
It is being estimated that up to a fifth of the working population carries out   3 ....
its duties at night – running hospitals and maintaining up power stations, for example. 4 ....
　　There is one problem: they have the same as biological clock   5 ....
as day workers. Night workers often have trouble sleeping through the   6 ....
day, and sometimes find it harder than to stay awake on their shift,   7 ....
which means mistakes are more likely to happen. Dr Lawrence Smith, a   8 ....
psychologist, discovered that among people who just carry out the   9 ....
same job, night workers suffered 20% more injuries than their day workers.   10 ....
　　He is now testing the theory that the light can be used to fool   11 ....
the human being body clock. The body clock resides in the hypothalamus,   12 ....
a cherry-sized small part of the brain, located behind the eyes, that   13 ....
regulates physiological processes such as body temperature and blood   14 ....
pressure over a every 24-hour cycle. The body clock appears to be   15 ....
influenced by light, because of one chemical at its disposal is sensitive to light.   16 ....

4 CONDITIONAL FORMS

Put the verbs in brackets into an appropriate form to complete these sentences. There is sometimes more than one correct answer.

1   If Alan (book) earlier, he (get) better seats for last night's performance.
2   As long as you (train) your voice, you (be able to) sing a wider range of music soon.
3   Jane (to be asked) to next month's reception, I am sure she (accept).
4   On condition that you (pay) by the end of the month, we (forward) the goods.
5   Sara (work) in Russia now if her visa (come) through in time.
6   If you see the red light (be) on in the studio, it (mean) they are recording.
7   Supposing Rob (not turn up) on time last night, you (wait)?
8   If I (travel) a lot these days, I always (get) tired.
9   'I'm so sorry to disturb you, Mr Nelson. It (be) better if I (call) back later?'
10 If she (take) the 10.30 train, she (arrive) at the hotel by now.
11 If you (like) to wait in reception, I (tell) Mrs Palmer you are here.
12 If you (work) late this evening, I (go) to the gym for an hour or two.

Total 24

5 PREFIXES AND SUFFIXES

Put the words in brackets in the correct form to complete these sentences.

1   If you are .... with the goods, please return them within 14 days. (satisfaction)
2   The director of the company was imprisoned once the .... dealings of the company were revealed. (legal)
3   His .... attitude set him apart from his colleagues and made him difficult to work with. (conform)
4   Her .... husband had the cheek to ask her for money. (faith)
5   Although Anne's daughter is 20, she's still very .... (mature)
6   The .... employee was sacked after he had been caught red-handed with his fingers in the till. (honest)
7   It's an .... rule that members of the sports club must take home all their equipment during the Christmas holidays. (write)
8   But for the .... climate, settlers would have plundered the treasures of the forest. (hospitable)
9   The tennis coach's .... remarks made the boy give up. (courage)
10 I don't know why you complain about her; her behaviour has been .... (reproach)

Total 10

6 WISH, IF ONLY, WOULD RATHER, IT'S TIME

Finish rewriting these sentences so they have the same meaning as the original.

1   We should go home; it's late.
    It's time ....
2   Jane wants to sit near the stage, not in the circle.
    Jane would rather ....
3   We've been waiting for the show to start for 15 minutes.
    We wish ....
4   I hope the circus comes to Glasgow.
    I wish ....
5   John hasn't got time to help us.
    If only ....
6   The children don't want to spend a summer's day watching a video.
    The children would rather ....
7   It's a pity this play is so boring.
    If only ....
8   Is it ever going to stop raining?
    I wish ....
9   I hate the way he dances like that.
    I wish ....
10 My father should have stopped smoking years ago.
    If only ....
11 It's 1pm. Let's have lunch!
    It's time ....
12 We should have had the tickets posted.
    I wish ....
13 It was a mistake to modernise the language of the play.
    I wish ....
14 It's terrible that Christine has got to do two shows a day.
    I wish ....
15 Suzanne should have her violin repaired.
    It's time ....

Total 15

7 ORDER OF ADJECTIVES

Put the adjectives in these descriptions into the most usual order.

1   17th-century vellum thick fascinating faded *manuscript*
2   dance colourful exciting new Brazilian *routine*
3   vegetarian huge highly successful restaurant American *chain*
4   fairy traditional British politically incorrect *story*
5   accurate computer colour detailed *analysis*
6   70s legal overly formal wordy *document*
7   plastic transparent A3 useful *folder*
8   hexagonal mahogany ornate theatre *box*
9   horror black and white realistic epic German *film*
10 avant-garde interior pinkish revolting *decor*

Total 10

11

1 VOCABULARY Idioms of crime

a 🔑 Match the two halves of these phrases and sayings.

1	crime	a	to pay Paul
2	he who pays the piper	b	and error
3	Jekyll	c	a judge
4	rob Peter	d	and dagger
5	by trial	e	does not pay
6	the law	f	and Hyde
7	as sober as	g	arm
8	to twist someone's	h	is an ass
9	the boys	i	in blue
10	cloak	j	calls the tune

b 🔑 What do the expressions in **a** mean? Choose a definition for each one.

the police
the legal system can be ridiculous
the person with financial control makes the decisions
to persuade someone
take money reserved for one thing and spend it on another
in the end, illegal dealings will not benefit you
mysterious, like in old films or novels
without having a drop of alcohol
trying to do something and, if it's wrong, trying again
a person with a very nice side and a very bad side to their character

2 READING

🔑 In the Coursebook you read about Philip Seldon, a man who runs courses to teach people how to get revenge! Read this extract from the same article and choose the best phrase, A–J, to complete each numbered gap (1–8). There are two extra phrases which do not fit.

A and distributed his 70 bottles of vintage wine to neighbourhood doorsteps

B such cases are unheard of in Britain

C who was given ten minutes to clear her desk

D the more satisfying the result

E especially if they belonged to her

F although it could be argued that the computers were joint property

G then walked out leaving only a message on her answerphone

H how else are you going to sleep at night

I getting even is not just an American dream, of course

J which is also his office

The constant stream of people lining up for Philip Seldon's get-even courses include Michelle, whose deep and murderous desire for vengeance on her cruel boyfriend has all the signs of a real-life *Fatal Attraction*. There is Martha [1] after 26 years in the same job. And there is Donna who wants to get even with the man who created a 'beautiful fantasy of marriage' [2]. Donna has already burned £100,000 worth of computer equipment belonging to her ex, and is eager to learn more tactics.

'I wouldn't advise anything destructive like that,' cautions Seldon. 'That might be illegal, [3]. You must stay within the law.'

Seldon, 56, masterminds his get-even classes from the Manhattan apartment [4]. He gives his lectures at local private colleges.

'I have always got even,' he says. 'It's so therapeutic. [5] when someone has hurt you? It's also quite simple really. You look for the weakness. Everyone has one. You plot and you move.'

[6] . There have been some spectacular acts of revenge in Britain, like Lady Moon, who shredded the arms of her husband's 32 Savile Row suits, poured six litres of white paint all over his BMW [7].

And a newsreader's wife who dumped his golfclubs and suits outside his mistress's front door.

Seldon admires that ploy. 'The important thing is not to think too small,' he says. 'Generally speaking, the grander the scheme, [8] . No sting is too ambitious, especially when it works.'

3 VOCABULARY Three-part phrasal verbs

a 🔑 **Match these three-part phrasal verbs (1–10) with their correct collocations (a–j) and definitions (i–x).**

1	face up to	a	flu
2	own up to	b	time
3	keep up with	c	the forensics department
4	get on to		
5	cut down on	d	responsibilities
6	run out of	e	breaking the vase
7	look up to	f	fatty food
8	go along with	g	clothes
9	go down with	h	her father
10	grow out of	i	his pace
		j	the plan

i	reduce/lessen
ii	have no more left
iii	accept and deal with
iv	admit
v	become too tall or big for
vi	catch an illness
vii	admire
viii	move at the same speed as
ix	accept
x	contact someone about something in particular

b 🔑 **Complete these sentences using an appropriate form of the verbs in the list.**

be   come (× 2)   get (× 2)   go
keep   miss   pick   settle

1 My daughter .... on at me until I gave in and bought her the trainers.
2 I was surprised he said he was born in the USA; I hadn't .... up on his accent.
3 Thanks for paying the bill; I'll .... up with you later.
4 It's a pity Susan was ill, she's had to .... out on the party.
5 Let's .... down to business.
6 The children are very quiet; I wonder what they .... up to?
7 Sophie's .... out in spots; I think she's got chicken pox.
8 He's .... in for a lot of criticism over his foreign policy.
9 Time for my dental appointment; I'll be glad to .... it over with.
10 I know I said I'd do it. But when it came to it I just couldn't .... through with it.

4 GRAMMAR Modal verbs

a 🔑 **Underline the modal verbs in these sentences and choose a meaning from the list to describe each one.**

necessity   inadvisability   obligation   probability (× 3)   no necessity   inability   unwillingness   possibility

1 These flowers are lovely; you shouldn't have.
2 I hope you don't mind. I've brought the dog along. Well, I couldn't just leave him on his own, could I?
3 It serves you right; you shouldn't have eaten so much.
4 I might have known you'd forget to post the letters.
5 You say someone phoned? Mmm, yes, that would have been Mark, probably.
6 You might have told me my buttons were undone!
7 Eleanor just wouldn't shut up.
8 The chocolate cake was so delicious I just had to have another piece.
9 Sorry I wasn't at home, but I really had to go to the bank.
10 Oh, look. There's an umbrella. Someone must have forgotten it.

b 🔑 🔑 **Listen to the sentences in a. Think about the meaning of the modal verbs and listen carefully to the intonation. Then choose a mood from the list to describe each speaker.**

speculation   contemplation   criticism   irritation   indulgence   pleasure   apologising   resignation   annoyance   presumption

c 🔑 **In this letter the modal verbs are used incorrectly. Can you correct them? There is sometimes more than one correct answer.**

Dear Jenny,

I'm very sorry to hear about your accident. I mustn't believe that the driver tried to drive off and leave you. If the policeman hadn't followed him he should never have been caught.

Jane told me that you're thinking of dropping the charges; Jenny you mightn't do that. It's important that people like him don't get away with it. He can be hoping you won't take it too seriously but honestly you must have been killed! I know you couldn't stay in hospital long but that's not the point.

You might employ a good solicitor; you can't worry about the cost. You are eligible for legal aid as you are a student. You can think I've got a cheek telling you what to do but it's not like that. I just mustn't stand by and say and do nothing.

Should you let me know what you decide to do? And of course I'll stand by you whatever you decide.

Best wishes

Jim

5 VOCABULARY Courtroom language

a 🗝️ Use these words to label the court scene.

clerk of the court   defendant   judge   jury   lawyer (for the defence/prosecution)
public gallery   the dock   usher   witness box

1 ....
2 ....
3 ....
4 ....
5 ....
6 ....
7 ....
8 ....
9 ....

b 🗝️ The verbs in these sentences are all associated with crime and punishment. Complete the sentences with the correct prepositions. Two sentences can also be written without a preposition. Which are they?

1 He was accused .... receiving stolen goods.
2 She was sentenced .... 180 hours of community service.
3 He was sued .... breach of contract.
4 She was awarded $1 million .... damages.
5 They were found guilty .... fraud.
6 The jury found .... favour .... Mrs Cox.
7 Her husband was paying $4,000 a month .... alimony.
8 She did it .... revenge.
9 The neighbour reported them .... disturbing the peace.
10 The judge reminded the witness that he was .... oath.

6 READING FOR PLEASURE

If you get into trouble while driving, you might like to think about some of these excuses people made for their accidents on insurance claim forms.

Coming home I drove into the wrong house and collided with a tree I don't have.

I had been driving for 40 years when I fell asleep at the wheel and had an accident.

The other car collided with mine without giving warning of its intention.

An invisible car came out of nowhere, struck my car and vanished.

I thought my window was down, but I found out it was up when I put my head through it.

To avoid hitting the bumper of the car in front I struck the pedestrian.

My car was legally parked as it backed into the other vehicle.

I collided with a stationary truck coming the other way.

I told the police I was not injured, but on removing my hat found that I had a fractured skull.

A truck backed through my windshield into my wife's face.

I was sure the old fellow would never make it to the other side of the road when I struck him.

A pedestrian hit me and went under my car.

The pedestrian had no idea which direction to run, so I ran over him.

The guy was all over the road. I had to swerve a number of times before I hit him.

I saw a slow-moving, sad-faced old gentleman as he bounced off the roof of my car.

I pulled away from the side of the road, glanced at my mother-in-law and headed over the embankment.

The indirect cause of the accident was a little guy in a small car with a big mouth.

In an attempt to kill a fly, I drove into a telephone pole.

I was thrown from my car as it left the road. I was later found in a ditch by some stray cows.

12

1 READING

Complete this extract from a book about money using one word to fill each gap.

Money is a taboo subject. Ask about sex, no problem. Ask about money and you are ¹.................... forbidden territory. Talking openly about it is often seen as embarrassing, even ².................... bad taste.

When I began talking to people about the meaning they ³.................... to money, I asked them to rate on a ⁴.................... of one to seven where they would ⁵.................... it in their lives. ⁶.................... said somewhere in the middle; relationships and health were far more important. I suspected I was not always ⁷.................... told the complete truth, so I stopped asking this ⁸.................... . The connection between the amount of money and possessions we desired and what we actually did with regard to them was ⁹.................... that simple.

Everyone wants to enjoy things ¹⁰.................... value is non-negotiable – ¹¹.................... good relationships with others, or the enjoyment of the beauty and wonder of the world – ¹².................... too often our view of money constrains ¹³.................... . There is an adage that goes 'A man's soul is slightly smaller than his mortgage', and ¹⁴.................... a soul produces a certain meanness. Meanness, in ¹⁵.................... , goes hand in hand ¹⁶.................... greed. These can be thought of in ¹⁷.................... of hunger and entitlement.

The hunger ¹⁸.................... money and possessions, ¹⁹.................... we can call greed, ²⁰.................... from a feeling of emptiness that threatens the integrity of the sense of existence. Acquiring more and more money and possessions can be an ²¹.................... to fill this void. Meanness – the refusal to ²².................... with money and possessions – can stem from a ²³.................... to give up anything deemed an essential buttress ²⁴.................... the sense of existence.

2 VOCABULARY Countable and uncountable nouns

a Match the two halves of these phrases.

1	a smudge of	a	sheep
2	a book of	b	cards
3	a stick of	c	thunder
4	a flock of	d	dust
5	a speck of	e	celery
6	a flash of	f	salt
7	a clap of	g	perfume
8	a dab of	h	lipstick
9	a deck of	i	matches
10	a pinch of	j	lightning

b Complete these sentences using words from the list. Sometimes there is more than one correct answer.

dash   flash   grain   handful   hint
item   load   pile   round   stretch

1 There isn't a .... of truth in what he said.
2 What a brilliant idea: a real .... of inspiration.
3 A .... of chilli sauce adds a zing to the salad dressing.
4 Despite the advance publicity only a .... of people turned up for the meeting.
5 Do you fancy a .... of golf at the weekend?
6 I've got a .... of work on my desk, waiting for me to do something about it.
7 There's a lovely .... of water between here and the forest.
8 The flavour's delicious; there's just a .... of lemon.
9 She was dressed to kill; every single .... of clothing was provocative.
10 Don't believe all that, it's a .... of rubbish.

3 LISTENING

You are going to hear part of a talk about the building of a new terminal for London's Heathrow airport and the environmental implications of air travel. Listen and complete these notes. You hear quite a lot of information in a short time, so be prepared!

REASONS FOR INCREASE IN AIR TRAVEL

Type of demand: 1 ....
Socio-economic change: 2 ....

COMPETITION
London surprising site for Europe's biggest airport because: 3 ....

Other European cities have: 4 ....
Effect on London if terminal not built: 5 ....

ENVIRONMENTAL ISSUES
New terminal built on: 6 ....
Wetland home to: 7 ....
Rare species found: 8 ....
Present site used as: 9 ....

EFFECTS ON LOCAL RESIDENTS
Effects greatest on people in: 10 .... and ....
Promises of British Aviation Authority: 11 ....
12 ....
13 ....

GLOBAL WARMING
Air travel consumes: 14 ....
Effect of global warming: 15 ....
IPCC recommendations: 16 ....
Britain's commitment: 17 ....
Britain's pollution: 18 ....
America's energy consumption: 19 USA = Britain × ....
20 USA = China × ....
21 USA = India × ....
Solution proposed by environmentalists: 22 ....

4 GRAMMAR The passive

Finish rewriting these sentences in the passive. The first one has been done for you.

1 They say they will increase the number of flights leaving from Heathrow.
It _is said the number of flights leaving Heathrow will be increased_ .

2 They believe the increase in air travel is due to holidaymakers.
It ....

3 They are dealing with the problem.
The problem ....
....

4 The doctor had already sent her the results of the tests.
She ....
....

5 Someone saw them entering the main building.
They ....
....

6 Her parents made her apologise.
She ....

7 They think she went abroad last night.
She ....
....

8 They say there was a disagreement between the surgeon and the theatre sister.
There ....
....

9 They have put off the meeting with the press twice now.
The meeting ....
....

10 You should make your cheques payable to The Clinic.
Cheques ....
....

11 The baby went to sleep once his mother had fed him.
Having ....

12 We can call the hunger for money and possessions 'greed'.
The hunger ....
....

5 VOCABULARY Idioms of clothing

Complete these sentences using the words in the list. Make any necessary changes to the words.

button buttonhole cloak coat collar dress hat shirt shoe skirt sock veil

1 She was .... to kill.
2 She was up to no good despite her .... of innocence.
3 The reason for this decision is .... in secrecy.
4 They .... round the issue instead of discussing it openly.
5 'I think you'd better .... your lip on that issue.'
6 The thief was .... by the police just as he was trying to leave with the stolen goods.

7 Some people can get really quite .... about moral issues.
8 I take my .... off to you for giving up smoking.
9 I wouldn't be in your .... for anything.
10 The test tube glass is .... with a special substance.
11 He .... his attacker in the jaw.
12 The Transport Minister left by the back door to avoid being .... by the protestors.

6 READING FOR PLEASURE The kiss

The kiss has always been a subject for hot debate in all sorts of entertainment, especially in films and novels. Did you know that there are only 14 kisses in all of Jane Austen's novels, and four of those are on the hand? Read on for more fascinating information.

LESS OF YOUR LIP: A HISTORY OF THE KISS

9 March, 1562: Kissing was banned in Naples, Italy, on penalty of death.

18 December, 1826: Dentists in New Jersey, USA, ordered people to stop kissing to prevent the spread of trench disease (a louse-borne disease common among soldiers in the trenches).

21 November, 1905: In Des Moines, Iowa, USA, Miss Elia Hamilton sued Hayden Marquis for $10,000 after he stole a kiss from her.

5 April, 1910: Kissing was banned on French railways on the grounds that it was delaying the trains.

25 December, 1913: A New York couple was arrested and fined $15 for kissing on the street on Christmas Day.

22 September, 1922: An 18-year-old sailor was fined in Stockholm for kissing his girlfriend in public. The magistrate declared it to have been 'obnoxious behaviour repulsive to public morals'.

10 January, 1993: Italy banned kissing while driving.

8 May, 1996: A man in Bangkok killed his wife after he saw another man giving her a kiss in a video of a relative's wedding. He said he lost his temper when she would not tell him who the man was.

27 August, 1996: A 39-year-old Egyptian woman was charged with assault after biting off the tongue of a 17-year-old boy. She had lured him into a painful embrace for spreading rumours about her alleged immoral behaviour.

8 October, 1996: The Board of Southwest Elementary School in Lexington, North Carolina, USA, voted to revise its sexual harassment policy after protests about its decision to punish a six-year-old boy for kissing a girl on the cheek. The boy said he did it 'because she is my friend'.

7 November, 1996: A woman in Edmonton, Canada, pleaded not guilty to charges of aggravated assault after she was accused of biting off her boyfriend's tongue, when he kissed her during an argument, and flushing it down the lavatory.

13

1 READING

One of the main 'feel-bad' factors of modern living is stress, especially if you live in a city and have a demanding job. Read this article about stress at work and choose a summary sentence, A–I, for each paragraph 1–7. There are two extra summary sentences which do not fit. The first one has been done for you.

A Illusion of control makes us feel better.
B Stress can show itself in different ways.
C Stress can be an expensive business.
D Diet is an important factor when considering stress.
E High-risk decision-making is better than no decision-making.
F A comfortable working environment reduces stress.
G The less control you have, the less you want to go to work.
H Be aware of your stress levels.
I Enforced inactivity can be just as stressful.

WORKING TO A FRENZY

1 C

Each year some 270,000 UK workers take time off because of work-related stress at a cost to the nation in sick pay, lost production and health care of over $7 billion. These figures would be much higher if the true toll of stress could be measured. Its effect on our personal life is often more profound. Small wonder that 'stress management' has become a growth industry or that children as young as four or five are being offered stress counselling at school.

2

A recent survey has confirmed what stress experts have long suspected: bosses suffer less stress than their subordinates. Only 9 per cent of junior managers looked forward to going to work and only 7 per cent felt they were in control of their jobs. The control factor is crucial. It has been demonstrated repeatedly that those who feel in control of their jobs and other areas of their lives are usually better able to control the ill effects of stress.

3

It's not just a life of limousines, langoustines and lackeys (compared with one of strap hanging and gulping sandwiches hastily at the desk) that makes bosses healthier – even with the supposedly high stress involved – than those who are not able to make decisions at all. That's why empowerment has become such a buzzword.

4

But there are many ways to give yourself or your employees the illusion of being in control, which seem to work. It has been shown that just having temperature controls on the wall (even if the heating/air conditioning is centrally controlled) makes workers happier about their environment, just as patients allowed to control their doses of pain-killers usually find they need less.

5

The stress of being unemployed, which inevitably gives a feeling of having no control over your life, is even worse and has been linked to a downward spiral of ill-health, as has enforced retirement. Recent American research has shown that elderly people allowed to control their own environment by living independently remain more physically and mentally active than those who go into 'homes' where they have to live to someone else's routine.

6

Stress can come in many guises. My stress might manifest itself in skin rashes and lethargy – yours in migraines and insomnia. While stress may not be the cause of many illnesses, it can certainly exacerbate them. It demonstrably weakens the immune system – less immunoglobulin A, which prevents colds and upper respiratory infections, is measured in the saliva of people when they are stressed than when they are relaxed.

7

One of the ways of being sensitive to your stress levels and stopping them from becoming destructively high is to be alert for the early warning signs – perhaps the beginnings of a cold, being tired all the time or suddenly accident prone. Learning to recognise your stress signals can help you to take appropriate action before things get out of hand. And don't think you're the only one to recognise them: the bitten nails and bags under the eyes are there for the world to see.

2 GRAMMAR The definite article

Answer these quiz questions, paying particular attention to the use of the definite article.

e.g. *Which is the largest desert in Africa?*
The Sahara.

1 Which continent is permanently frozen?
2 Which large river flows through London?
3 Name the large group of islands whose capital is Manila.
4 In which country can you find the Pyramids?
5 Which mountain chain runs along the west coast of South America?
6 Name the desert covering much of Mongolia and northern China.
7 What's the capital of Turkey?
8 What's the longest river in South America?
9 Which city in Australia has a famous opera house?
10 Which New York street is associated with the financial world?
11 Which ocean lies between America and Europe?
12 What's the highest mountain in the world?
13 Which star is 150,000,000km from the Earth?
14 What's the world's highest lake?
15 Which US state is Hollywood in?

3 LISTENING

a You are going to hear a guest speaker talking about a phenomenon called Murphy's Law. Listen and, according to what you hear, decide whether these statements are true or false. Write T for true and F for false.

1 It's not just a matter of chance when things go wrong. ☐
2 In the past most scientists believed incidences of Murphy's Law were just stories perpetuated in modern culture. ☐
3 A paperback book always lands face-down on the floor. ☐
4 Laws of physics can explain why toast tends to land butter-side down. ☐
5 Many cases have a rational explanation. ☐
6 Research into how queues move has been too random to prove anything. ☐
7 The length of the queue determines how fast it moves. ☐
8 It is unlikely that a second lost sock will be the odd one which had been left in the drawer. ☐

b Match these words and expressions (1–10), used by the guest speaker in a, to their correct definitions (a–j).

1 rummaging   a unwillingness to co-operate, deliberate awkwardness
2 vexations   b based on individuals' accounts
3 flukes   c chance happenings, usually positive
4 urban myth   d searching for something among a lot of other things in a careless or hurried way
5 barring   e thin cord
6 anecdotal   f in favour of
7 random   g excepting
8 cussedness   h things causing annoyance or worry
9 stacked towards i a popular story in modern culture
10 string   j without definite plan, pattern or purpose

4 VOCABULARY Expressions with *do*

In the Coursebook, you studied some expressions with *make*. Now use an English–English dictionary to look up the meaning of these expressions with *do*.

1 *This is doing my head in.
2 Do or die.
3 We did well out of the deal.
4 It isn't done.
5 *Nothing doing.
6 That'll do.
7 I can't do without that.
8 She did me out of £50.
9 *I'm done in.
10 *Do your own thing.

*informal expressions

5 PRONUNCIATION Silent letters

a Which letter(s) in these words are often not pronounced?

e.g. *staggering*

1 omelette
2 evening
3 business
4 marriage
5 every
6 different
7 usually
8 restaurant
9 secretary
10 Wednesday
11 awfully
12 aspirin
13 extraordinary
14 separate

b Mark the stressed syllable in the words in a.

e.g. *'staggering*

c Listen and repeat the words in a.

6 VOCABULARY Parts of the whole

Label these illustrations using words from the lists.

1 petal   stamen   stem   leaf
2 bud   branch   trunk   roots   twig   bark
3 segment   skin/peel/rind   pip   pith
4 kernel   shell
5 white   yolk   shell

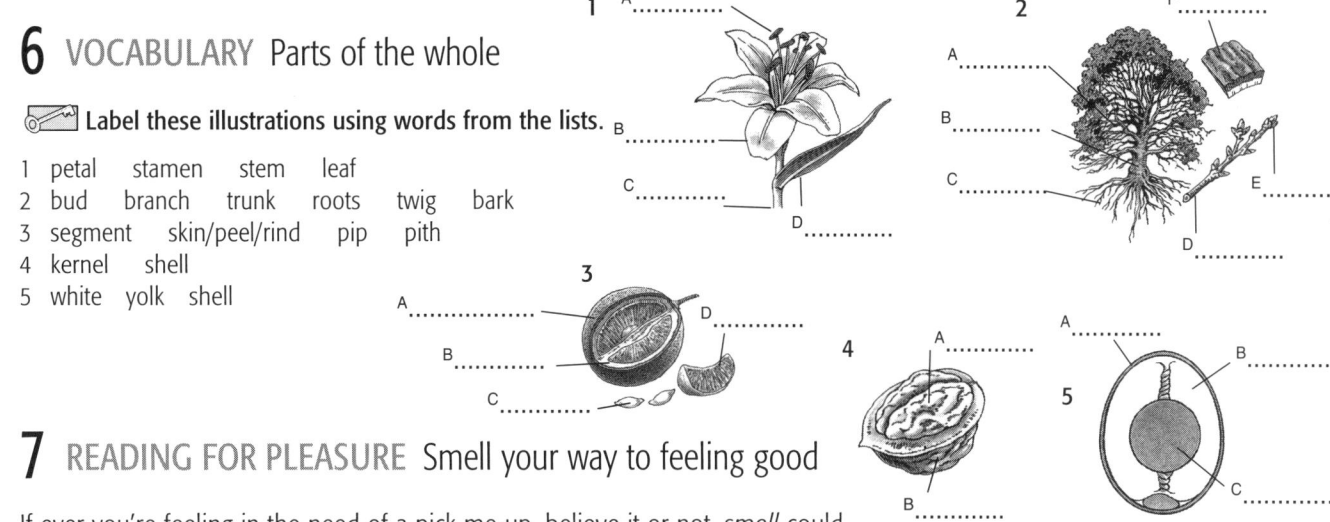

7 READING FOR PLEASURE Smell your way to feeling good

If ever you're feeling in the need of a pick-me-up, believe it or not, *smell* could make you feel pampered, relaxed or refreshed. Read on and all will be revealed.

Classroom aroma

Paul Power comments on the use of aromatherapy oils in the classroom.

Over a number of years research has been able to demonstrate that essential oils can have a profound effect, not only on the physiology but also on the emotional and spiritual plane. To give a few examples – orange is useful for those who have become tired of meeting obstacles and have become frustrated and perhaps lazy. Bergamot is appropriate for someone who sets high standards, is over-determined and perhaps cross and critical of others. Myrrh can be used for someone who has for the moment lost confidence in their abilities to succeed or lemongrass may help a person who finds it difficult to assert themselves or express their wishes and purposes. Juniper would be suitable for anyone suffering from stress or of a nervous disposition.

So how can we start using essential oils in the classroom?

Let's start with some methods of application.

1 A bowl of water with added oils can be placed near a radiator.
2 A small towel can be saturated in water. This is then wrung out and the drops of oil shaken onto the towel. The towel is then draped over the radiator which will release the scent into the room.
3 A plant spray can be filled with water, oils added and the mixture liberally sprayed round the room.
4 Various vaporisers and burners can be bought. Many of them use electric power and so will not contravene fire regulations.

Before using oils always check for contra-indications as a small number of oils should not be used in cases of pregnancy, high blood pressure, etc.

Here are some of my own recipes you might like to try out in various situations.

1 To ward off germs and colds so easily passed around the classroom:
3 drops of Lavender
2 drops of Eucalyptus
2 drops of Pine

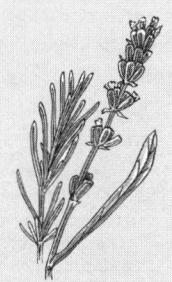

2 For exam classes beginning to feel the stresses and strains of the course:
3 drops of Bergamot
3 drops of Geranium
3 drops of Jasmine

3 To calm down excited students!
3 drops of Camomile
2 drops of Sandalwood
2 drops of Rose

4 When students seem apathetic and unwilling to participate freely:
2 drops of Grapefruit
2 drops of Rosemary
2 drops of Ginger

5 For classes that find it hard to concentrate:
3 drops of Cedarwood
2 drops of Frankincense
2 drops of Ylang ylang

6 Just to provide a pleasant classroom fragrance:
3 drops of Lemon
2 drops of Bergamot
2 drops of Lavender

14

1 READING

a 🔑 For many people the computer has meant a significant change in lifestyle. Read this article about people becoming addicted to using computers. Four sentences have been removed from the article. Choose from sentences A–F the one which fits each gap (1–4). There are two extra sentences which do not fit.

A Nearly half work longer hours or take home work in an effort to keep up.
B It takes hours to find the information when you had intended to spend only a few minutes with your PC.
C Another woman slept with her PC.
D He said electronic delivery of data was growing.
E The survey of 1,000 people in the UK, US, Germany, Ireland, Singapore and Hong Kong shows that 53 per cent of managers 'crave' information.
F There are growing fears for the health of children who already encounter it.

Concern over the office cyberjunkies* who OD* on IT*

Forget smack. The drug of the moment, being used by millions day and night, is legal, and costs little more than the price of a phone call.

Managers stay late at the office to use it. 1 ☐ And 75 per cent of people polled about its dangers warn that the addiction is getting worse.

Information is the drug and a new generation of dataholics are the addicts. A survey carried out by Reuters suggests thousands of people are becoming addicted to information and that many crave more of it to the detriment of social and family life. 2 ☐ 54 per cent admit to a 'high' when they find the right data.

One in three managers believes their colleagues are obsessed with gathering information, while three-quarters believe information can become addictive. Nearly three-quarters say they have less job satisfaction and suffer greater tension with their colleagues due to overdoses of information, while two out of every five are so addicted that they look for work-related information even when on holiday.

Michael Foster, Reuters director of business information, said electronic delivery of data was growing and was additional to the traditional paper and speech. More than half the managers said they could not cope with the amount of information they were sent. 3 ☐

Dr Mark Griffiths, a senior lecturer specialising in addiction at Nottingham Trent University, said the Internet may be responsible. Competitive pressures and job insecurity made people feel they had to stay up to date at all costs.

Net use could produce similar changes in the body 'as occurs with pathological gamblers, including heightened adrenalin, endorphin and cerebral spinal fluid'.

Dr Griffiths said a woman has been found guilty of neglecting her small children as she spent all her time surfing the Net. 4 ☐

Cyberjunkies are advised to go on-line only at certain times of day, to avoid on-screen junk mail and to strive to cut down time at the computer. And they must recognise the limitations of the technology.

*cyberjunkies are people addicted to using personal computers, especially the Internet
*OD means overdose, which normally means to take too much of a drug
*IT means information technology

b 🔑 What do these words mean?

1 dataholic
2 alcoholic
3 chocoholic
4 workaholic
5 junk mail
6 junk food

2 GRAMMAR Inversion

a 🔑 Finish rewriting these sentences so they have the same meaning as the original.

1 There is so much demand for Internet services that many people are finding it difficult to get on-line.
   Such ....
2 If I had realised how long it would take, I would never have started.
   Had ....
3 It was only when we went to the USA that we realised the extent of PC use.
   Only ....
4 Jane has changed her lifestyle and abandoned her old friends.
   Not only ....
5 We didn't suspect at all that she had been neglecting her children.
   Little ....
6 As soon as we got new computers, all the students enrolled for the IT course.
   No sooner ....
7 I was never told how to use it.
   At no time ....
8 The waiter is coming.
   Here ....
9 The boy jumped up.
   Up ....
10 Michael doesn't want to go and his brother doesn't either.
   Michael doesn't want to go and neither ....

b 🗝 Correct these sentences if necessary. Tick any sentences which are already correct.

1 Scarcely entered I the room when the butler appeared.
2 There go the office staff, back to work after lunch.
3 My line manager lives in a very stylish part of town, as do all the other managers.
4 Not only makes you the computer tired, but it also wastes a lot of time.
5 Only the British treat animals better than their children.
6 'I'd rather my boss didn't comment on my hairstyle.'
   'So I would.'
7 Down the stairs tumbled she like a rag doll.
8 There is sitting the designer, Vivienne Westwood.
9 Such was the reaction that we withdrew the product.
10 On no account must you sign any of the papers.

3 READING AND VOCABULARY

🗝 Read this extract from an article about Tamagotchis and choose the word, A, B, C or D, which best fits each gap. The first one has been done for you.

e.g. *0 = B*

	A	B	C	D
0	means	translates	transfers	implies
1	displayed	monitored	exhibited	called
2	thus	lest	unlike	as
3	sounds	tinkles	clinks	poses
4	disaffection	complaisance	deception	complaint
5	portions	injections	measurements	helpings
6	substance	implication	evidence	relation
7	sham	false	fake	spurious
8	let off	undertaken	set out	launched
9	raising	generating	elevating	stocking
10	let	put	part	fall

TAMAGOTCHI

The Tamagotchi, which ⁰............................ as 'cute little egg', is a key-chain computer game about the size and shape of an egg. The game starts when an egg ¹............................ on the screen hatches and a chicken is born. The owner then uses three tiny buttons to feed, play with, clean up after and discipline it. ²............................ most video games, which are over in a few minutes, this one can go on for days.

With proper care, the chicken grows. If the owner forgets to feed it, it ³............................ a loud 'peep, peep, peep' of ⁴............................ . If the chicken makes a mess and the owner doesn't clean it up, then the chicken peeps even louder. The owner can tickle it with the press of a button,

or take its temperature and give it ⁵............................ of 'medicine' if it seems ill.

Ignore the chicken, drop it on the subway, forget it at home or neglect to tickle it often enough, and it will grow sickly and mean-looking. Eventually it will die. Game over. The ⁶............................ is that you are a loser. You can't even keep a ⁷............................ chicken alive.

More than 500,000 Tamagotchis were sold in the first two months after this virtual pet was ⁸............................ by Bandai, the huge Japanese toymaker famous for Power Rangers. But unlike many toys, Tamagotchis are not just for the young. Middle-aged businessmen play with them on the subway. Some companies are ⁹............................ Tamagotchi chickens as a group project; meetings stop when the chicken peeps for its lunch. An actress being interviewed on a television talk show accidently dropped a Tamagotchi out of her pocket; she explained with an embarrassed smile that she couldn't ¹⁰............................ with the chicken because it needed her constant care.

4 VOCABULARY Compound words

a 🗝 Match the two halves of these words to make 10 common compounds. Use an English–English dictionary to help you. Do not make phrasal verbs like *cut off*. There is a hyphen for words which are hyphenated.

1	body	2	cut-	3	dumb	4	get	5	make
6	scrap	7	smoke	8	telling-	9	terror-	10	weak-

a	shift	b	away	c	guard	d	off	e	stricken
f	kneed	g	book	h	throat	i	screen	j	struck

b 🔑 Complete these sentences using the compound words in **a**.

1   I was .... when I heard that I had won the award.
2   The thieves used a high performance vehicle as their .... car.
3   Her mother was really angry and gave her a .... in front of everyone.
4   Most famous people have .... , you know.
5   She's so .... she's bound to give in to him.
6   There were dozens of .... filled with photos and newspaper clippings.
7   Working as a secretary was just a .... for her industrial espionage.
8   We were .... as huge waves came crashing in from the sea.
9   The competition is .... now in the fashion business.
10 As the rooms were not ready, we used .... accommodation at the back
    of the building.

5 READING FOR PLEASURE

How to pack a suitcase

There's nothing to it, surely?

There most certainly is. Pack a case badly and you will arrive with crumpled suits and creased trousers, then spend the rest of your holiday searching for an ironing board or looking like a vagrant.

Where do I start?

Buy the right case. Something solid and anonymous with a toughened shell. Not a flimsy designer holdall that will attract lingering looks from thieves and casual kicks from airport baggage handlers.

Then just throw in all my clothes?

Wait for it. The first rule of packing is to make sure you have properly *unpacked* after your last trip: shake out the case and air it thoroughly, preferably in the garden on a fine day. A single sock or handkerchief, if left in there for long enough, can give a suitcase a musty odour.

Then I can start packing?

Hold your horses. First you need some acid-free tissue paper. This will keep your clothes clean and act as a shock absorber to prevent them becoming creased. It must be white: any other colour might stain damp clothes.

What do I do with this paper?

Line your case with it, then place two sheets between each layer of clothes and stuff some more of it into the arms and shoulders of jackets and between the pleats of ladies' skirts. You will need about twelve sheets per case.

Sounds expensive.

It's worth it, and you can reuse the paper two or three times. When you get home, iron it on medium heat and fold it carefully for future trips.

Can I pack my clothes in any order?

Dear me, no. According to Ivor Spencer, who runs a school for butlers in south London, trousers should go in first. Remove belts and empty the pockets, then lay them across the base of the suitcase so that the waistband is in the centre and the legs dangle over the rim. A second pair can be laid across the opposite side of the case so that the two waistbands meet in the middle. The remaining clothes are then laid out flat with the minimum of folding and the trouser legs wrapped across the top – with extra tissue around the knees – to make a neat parcel.

Is this really the best way?

It is the *proper* way.

I was always told to roll up T-shirts and trousers.

That might crease them. But, if you insist on being different, you could fold your clothes into square parcels, wrap them in plastic bags, then slot them into the case like building blocks with plenty of layers of tissue paper throughout.

I usually put in my shoes first.

Not recommended. Slip them into shoe bags to stop the polish rubbing on to shirts or dresses then pack them with the soles facing up. Use plastic shoetrees rather than wooden ones (they are lighter).

I don't have any shoetrees.

Shame on you! In that case, improvise with one or two pairs of socks folded and pushed into the toe of each shoe. Don't roll socks – they will lose their elasticity.

Can I roll my ties?

Yes, but inside out. Silk shirts and blouses should also be folded inside out. Jackets go in last, folded in half from top to bottom, with another layer of tissue paper under the fold and a quick check that the vents at the back are not going to get creased.

What if I still arrive with creased clothes?

Use the old steaming method. Run the shower very hot until the bathroom is thick with steam, then hang the offending item from the hook behind the door.

And leave it for half an hour or so?

Not unless you want it to be ruined. Two minutes will usually suffice, then remove it and hang it up in your hotel bedroom.

And my travel iron?

Leave it at home. It need travel no more.

15

1 READING AND VOCABULARY

Read this book extract about personal space and choose the word, A, B, C or D, which best fits each gap. The first one has been done for you.

e.g. *0 = A*

PERSONAL SPACE

We all have an instinctive ⁰............ for personal space. Besides attempts to retain privacy which are efforts to ¹............ physically or psychologically from the social world into a private world, city dwellers have had to ²............ and make changes to their personal space. Personal space is a psychological construct ³............ to the physical distance or boundary we all attempt to ⁴............ between ourselves and the people around us. In general, this space is roughly circular but with a larger space in front of us than behind. We find ourselves being comfortable with a ⁵............ distance between ourselves and others around us and will move to ⁶............ this distance. The exact distance is ⁷............ upon a number of individual, social and, particularly in the city, situational factors. In the city we find it difficult to keep people out of our space bubbles and to escape.

In the city there are ⁸............ situations where the general rules of personal space are ⁹............ . Any trip on a crowded underground train or standing in a bus ¹⁰............ close physical contact with strangers.

The city has created a different culture of personal space by ¹¹............ many situations as ones where personal space will be invaded and the ¹²............ of flight is removed. Consequently, city dwellers have developed finely ¹³............ skills to deal with situations where ¹⁴............ is so close as to be at an intimate level with strangers. It is quite acceptable to be in close physical contact with strangers in these situations but we still use classic strategies of non-verbal signals to create a ¹⁵............ between ourselves and others. We withdraw our bodies, turn away from people, try to avoid skin-to-skin ¹⁶............ and apologise when our hands touch. Turning away is a technique that we know reduces the extent of our personal space in a forward direction. City people have become skilled at ¹⁷............ a newspaper or book between themselves and others around them.

We also avoid eye contact as this is a signal to initiate a conversation. Instead, in the absence of a book or newspaper, we adopt the middle distance ¹⁸............ , an unfocused steady look across the crowd or in elevators at the indicator as the lift moves.

0	A	need	B	appeal	C	search	D	request
1	A	revert	B	dissent	C	withdraw	D	recede
2	A	substitute	B	confirm	C	transform	D	adapt
3	A	demonstrating	B	meaning	C	indicating	D	referring
4	A	maintain	B	support	C	sustain	D	operate
5	A	descriptive	B	particular	C	special	D	attentive
6	A	adjust	B	imitate	C	regulate	D	order
7	A	subject	B	dependent	C	owing	D	founded
8	A	countless	B	untold	C	interminable	D	boundless
9	A	defeated	B	subjected	C	quelled	D	overwhelmed
10	A	concerns	B	comprises	C	involves	D	contains
11	A	determining	B	defining	C	itemising	D	quantifying
12	A	option	B	selection	C	adoption	D	designation
13	A	honed	B	sharpened	C	edged	D	ground
14	A	nearness	B	propinquity	C	proximity	D	vicinity
15	A	hindrance	B	stockade	C	barricade	D	barrier
16	A	joining	B	contact	C	clash	D	touch
17	A	interposing	B	stationing	C	assigning	D	locating
18	A	peek	B	leer	C	stare	D	glance

2 VOCABULARY Prepositions

Complete these sentences with a preposition.

1　Maggie had to confide .... someone as the problem seemed to be getting worse.
2　City life can result .... a feeling of loneliness.
3　He insisted .... helping her move into her new flat.
4　Some people seem to boast .... their material possessions all the time.
5　I've decided to confront my neighbour .... the fact that his music keeps me awake all night.
6　We were distracted .... listening to the talk by some people chattering at the back of the hall.
7　Congratulations .... winning the prize!
8　I think he was hinting .... something a little more intimate.
9　The company will provide you .... the special clothing you will need.
10　It's obvious who is going to benefit .... this.

3 LISTENING

You are going to hear an expert talking about personal space. You might like to read the text in 1 again before you listen. Then listen and complete the chart, according to what you hear.

Personal space				
Type of personal space	'intimate distance'	4	7	10
Relationships	1	family and friends, business colleagues	8	11
Distances	2	5	9	12
Comment	3	6	status and decorum retained	—

4 GRAMMAR Indirect speech

a　Rewrite these sentences using indirect speech and beginning with *He/She said/told/asked*.

e.g. *'Did you eat a lot of fish dishes when you lived in Japan?'*
***He asked** me if I had eaten a lot of fish dishes when I lived in Japan.*

1　'I feel very uncomfortable talking to John now because he is standing too close.'
2　'If we had observed people's behaviour in cities, we would have got very different results.'
3　'City dwellers have developed finely honed skills to deal with crowds.'
4　'Unless they adapt to the culture, they will find it difficult to get on here.'
5　'You might be able to avoid eye contact by reading a book.'
6　'Do people shake hands with each other in Japan?'
7　'What do people do in your country when they meet for the first time?'
8　'Can you meet us tomorrow?'
9　'Don't look at me like that. You are making me feel guilty.'
10　'Would you open the window, please?'

b　Finish rewriting these sentences using indirect speech.

1　'I wouldn't take the underground late at night if I were you.'
　　She advised ....

2　'Don't forget to wear a dark suit. It's quite a formal meeting.'
　　He reminded ....

3　'Yes, I can see that I've made a mistake.'
　　Frank accepted ....

4　'And there will be two more for dinner.'
　　She added ....

5　'I think it will cost about £5,000.'
　　He estimated ....

6　'Would you like to go to the opening?'
　　He invited ....

7　'I tell you, I haven't moved it.'
　　Emma insisted ....

8　'I think you should study sociology.'
　　She advised ....

9　'Why don't you and Philip try the new Italian restaurant?'
　　He suggested ....

10　'Make sure you don't sit next to Pat, she's such a bore.'
　　He warned ....

5 VOCABULARY Things people can study

a 🔊 In the Coursebook you read about the palaeontologist, Louis Leakey. *Palaeontology* is the study of extinct and fossilised animals or plants. What are these *-ologies* the study of? Choose a definition for each one.

arachnology   archaeology   astrology   campanology   entomology   etymology   geology   graphology
horology   lepidopterology   meteorology   mythology   oceanology   phrenology   psychology   seismology
sociology   theology   toxicology   vulcanology

1   the origins and historical development of words
2   the movements of planets, etc., and their influence on people's lives
3   spiders
4   the human mind
5   volcanoes
6   technology/economics relating to human use of the sea
7   measuring time, clocks and watches
8   insects
9   history/culture of ancient societies by examining the remains of buildings/objects
10   the size and shape of the cranium to ascertain character
11   human societies and relationships between the groups
12   earthquakes
13   rocks and soil to find out about structure, origin, history
14   moths and butterflies
15   bells and bell ringing
16   poisons
17   fables, parables and allegories
18   the weather for forecasting
19   religion
20   handwriting

b 🔊 Mark the stressed syllable in the words in **a**.

e.g. *arach'nology*

c   Practise saying the words you want to remember.

6 LISTENING FOR PLEASURE

Limericks 🔊

There was a young lady of Venice
Who used hard-boiled eggs to play tennis.
　　When they said: 'It is wrong,'
　　She replied, 'Go along:
You don't know how prolific my hen is.'

There was an old fellow of Cosham
Who took out his false teeth to wash 'em.*
　　But his wife said: 'Dear Jack,
　　If you don't put them back,
I will tread on your teeth and squash 'em.'

*'em = them

There was a young lady of Leek
Who had fifty proposals a week.
　　Though she never grew tired
　　Of being admired,
She was often too sleepy to speak.
　　　　Randall Davies

There was an old dame of Malacca
Who smoked such atrocious tobacca,*
　　That when tigers came near
　　They trembled with fear,
And didn't attempt to attack her.

*normally spelt tobacco;
changed here for the rhyme

There was once a young man of East Sheen,
Who grew so remarkably lean,
　　So flat and compressed,
　　That his back touched his chest,
And sideways he couldn't be seen.

Test of Units 11–15

1 MODAL VERBS

Choose the most suitable modal verb in italics to complete these sentences.

e.g. People *shouldn't/can't* drive a car until they are 17 in Britain. (*can't* is better because it's against the law)

1 James *can't/couldn't* get out of bed for two weeks after the accident.
2 I don't think you *should/could* have lost your temper like that.
3 We *needn't/mustn't* have booked a table; the restaurant's nearly empty.
4 *Might/Could* you help me with these boxes?
5 He *could/should* well have told the truth.
6 I *couldn't/shouldn't* possibly accept such a gift.
7 We *don't have to/mustn't* pay full price because we're students.
8 I suppose we *might/could* as well tell you everything.
9 We *didn't need to go/needn't have gone* to the police station because they didn't help us at all.
10 Odile *mustn't have gone/didn't need to go* to the hospital because she felt much better.
11 That woman *should/must* be his wife from the way she's keeping her eye on him.
12 You *shouldn't/can't* have seen Robin in the cinema; he's in the USA on business.
13 There *can/could* be severe weather at times in this region.
14 You *mustn't/shouldn't* be reading in this poor light.
15 She *should/might* well inherit a lot of money.

	Total 15

2 PREPOSITIONS

Complete these sentences with the correct prepositions.

1 She tore up her husband's clothes .... revenge. (2 points)
2 The company was sued .... unfair dismissal.
3 The gang was accused .... armed robbery.
4 He was found guilty .... blackmail.
5 If you tell a lie while you are .... oath, that is perjury.
6 She was sentenced .... five years in jail.
7 The jury found .... favour .... the defendant. (2 points)
8 She will get a fortune .... alimony after her divorce.

	Total 10

3 WORD STRESS

Mark the stressed syllables in these words.

e.g. *compen'sation*

1 legality
2 judgemental
3 precedent
4 confiscation
5 criminology
6 forensics
7 eligibility
8 defendant
9 prosecutor
10 accusatory

	Total 10

4 THREE-PART PHRASAL VERBS

Complete these sentences with a suitable three-part phrasal verb.

e.g. Jack has *split up with* his girlfriend.

1 My brother's going to .... promotion next month. I hope he gets it.
2 The trip was wonderful; it .... all my expectations.
3 Mary seems on top of the world. I .... it that great new boyfriend she's got.
4 I don't know how Philip .... his son's music blaring out all day long.
5 I've missed two weeks of lessons so it's going to take me a few days to .... the rest of the class.
6 How well do you .... your new boss? He seems very cold.
7 I .... a competition last month and I've just heard I've won a car!
8 Work's been so busy lately, I'm really .... my holiday.
9 We need more people to help with the play. Can I .... you .... sewing costumes?
10 Mr Simson .... a shock. Just wait till he sees the sales figures.

	Total 10

5 THE PASSIVE

Rewrite these sentences using the passive form.

e.g. *The police have arrested a man in connection with their enquiries.*
A man has been arrested by the police in connection with their enquiries.

1   They are running tests on the new machinery this week.
2   They produce high-quality electronic goods in Korea.
3   They must receive the application form before the end of the month.
4   They thought he had left the country.
5   They made her take another driving test.
6   We expect they will announce the winner next Monday.
7   They believe her to be a talented musician.
8   They say young men are the worst drivers.
9   They asked me to be waiting in the foyer.
10 They allowed us to enter the palace.

Total 10

6 INVERSION

Finish rewriting these sentences so they have the same meaning as the original.

e.g. The meal was so delicious that I will remember it for ever.
So _delicious was the meal that I will remember it for ever_ .

1   If you need any further information, please do not hesitate to contact us.
Should _____ .
2   The Prime Minister has several bodyguards and his ministers do too.
The Prime Minister has several bodyguards, as
_____ .
3   Nicki runs a successful company and she also manages to look after her four children.
Not only _____ .
4   As soon as the concert started there was an electrical fault and the lights went out.
No sooner _____ .
5   I didn't imagine for one moment that anyone would object.
Not for one moment _____ .
6   A Ming vase was standing on the hall table.
On the hall table _____ .
7   The opera had hardly started when the principal singer fainted.
Hardly _____ .
8   I have never had such a good time.
Never _____ .
9   He was so embarrassed that he left the room.
Such _____ .
10 We didn't realise at all that he was her father.
Little _____ .

Total 10

7 COUNTABLE AND UNCOUNTABLE NOUNS

Complete these phrases.

e.g. a _batch_ of cakes

1   a _____ of wool
2   a _____ of grass
3   a _____ of grapes
4   a _____ of garlic
5   a _____ of perfume
6   a _____ of fish
7   a _____ of cows
8   a _____ of beer
9   a _____ of film
10 a _____ of paper

Total 10

8 COMPOUND WORDS

Complete these sentences with a suitable compound word.

e.g. Susan hates having her photo taken; she's _camera-shy_ .

1   He said he was interested in historical buildings but that was just a _____ for planning the robbery.
2   Because of the kidnapping threat he has hired a _____ to protect his family.
3   The seaside resort made most of its money from _____ who came down from London.
4   I kept a _____ of my three-month stay in Australia. It's full of leaflets, tickets and photos.
5   The new _____ computers will be marvellous especially for people who suffer from arthritis or who have any other problems with their hands.
6   Martin couldn't say a word, he was _____ by the news.
7   It's time for the concert to start but some seats are still empty so we'd better wait a few more minutes for the _____ .
8   The robbers were seen leaving in a silver _____ car.
9   I fear she might think me _____ for giving in so easily to his decision.
10 This _____ fence will do to keep the animals in until I have time to put up something more permanent.

Total 10

Answers and tapescripts

1 VOCABULARY

a

1 Advanced level examinations: usually taken at the age of 18 at the end of secondary school
2 Master of Arts/Science/Business Administration
3 General Certificate of Secondary Education: usually taken at the age of about 16 at secondary school
4 Bachelor of Arts/Science
5 Doctor of Philosophy

b

The order is: 5, 2, 4, 1, 3.

c

1 PA (personal address)
2 GP (general practitioner)
3 Euro MP (Member of the European Parliament)
4 VIP (very important person)
5 VAT (value added tax)
6 DIY (do-it-yourself)
7 PM (Prime Minister)
8 HQ (headquarters)
9 PC (personal computer)
10 IQ (intelligence quotient)

2 GRAMMAR

a

Verbs which are followed by the infinitive: agree, appear, beg, decide, expect, hope, manage, offer, permit, persuade, pretend, refuse.
Verbs which are followed by the -ing form: avoid, deny, fancy, give up, mind, practise, risk, suggest.

b The corrections are in bold.

Dear Mr Burns

I am very pleased **to confirm** your forthcoming travel arrangements and, with regard to this matter, enclose your invoice and financial statement. I trust you will find these **to be** in order, but do not hesitate **to contact** me should you have any queries or concerns.

As settlement was made **in** full **at** the time of booking, no **further** payment is due.

If you are travelling abroad, it is your responsibility **to ensure** that you and all **members** of your party have a **valid** passport and any necessary visas. If you are **in** any doubt, please do not hesitate **to contact** me.

We shall of course be delighted **to supply** your foreign exchange requirements and **help** you with any queries you may have relating to car hire, airport hotel accommodation and airport car parking.

May I take this **opportunity to thank** you once again for booking with Worldwide Tours.

Yours **sincerely**

C. Garcia

C. Garcia

Encs: invoice
      financial statement

---

3 READING

a

2 D   3 E   4 C   5 A   6 B

b

1 the most important person in the family
2 entered
3 a comfortable place
4 draped in material and decorations
5 completely removed any obvious sign of (its) use
6 to put on show the objects which signify someone's prestige and importance
7 people who live in one place and travel regularly to another place for work
8 the structure itself of our cities
9 a village where people live, away from their place of work
10 an outlying residential area with no interesting characteristics
11 an area of a city where living conditions are poor

4 VOCABULARY

a

1 registered as unemployed and receiving money from the government
2 a short intensive course which teaches the most important things
3 not employed by one particular company but selling services to any organisation that wants to buy
4 the time during which someone is assessed at the beginning of a new job before their employment is confirmed
5 reducing the number of employees
6 a system which allows employees to vary the time that they start or finish work provided that an agreed total number of hours per week/month is spent at work
7 unemployed because a company no longer has work to offer
8 natural ability
9 according to how much is used
10 exhausted
11 more than the usual price
12 normal price

b

Ask your teacher to check the sentences or paragraph you have written.

5 LISTENING

a

1 banker   2 lawyer   3 TV newsreader   4 engineer

Chemist and doctor are not mentioned.

b

1 accounts, balances, statements
2 practice, partners, clients, case
3 headlines, auto-cue
4 developing, (measuring) instrument

c

1 resigned   2 indignant   3 embarrassed   4 incredulous

1 Well, we might as well face it. Companies these days are always looking for ways to cut costs, and we're no exception. We've started sending a significant portion of our computer work to Asia, for example. They rewrite software programs for us whenever we need new systems for accounts, balances and statements. Even a lot of the

routine work is done there now and there's nothing we can do about it. When we come into work the next day, because of the time difference, a lot of the work has been done for us.

2　Yes, it's quite a large practice, with about 17 partners. And can you credit it? Even now, going into the 21st century, we get some usually rather elderly clients, who, when they're told that *Ms Crawley* will handle their case, demand a male partner. I've had to work hard to get where I am, probably harder than some of the male partners, and then to be told … well, it's a professional insult!

3　I'd already started and had got through the headlines and was just starting on the main item, when the auto-cue started going berserk. It started scrolling up much too fast and I couldn't keep up with it. I felt myself getting redder and redder as I furiously signalled for it to be slowed down. But then it went too slow. I just didn't know how to handle it. I felt a right twit.

4　Recently we've been developing a measuring instrument for checking the purity of water and we've come up with this very sophisticated and sensitive instrument. We wanted to put it to the acid test and test it with what is supposedly the purest water you can get. Well, anyway, when we got this water and tested it, it was *full* of bugs. I couldn't believe my eyes.

6　PRONUNCIATION

b

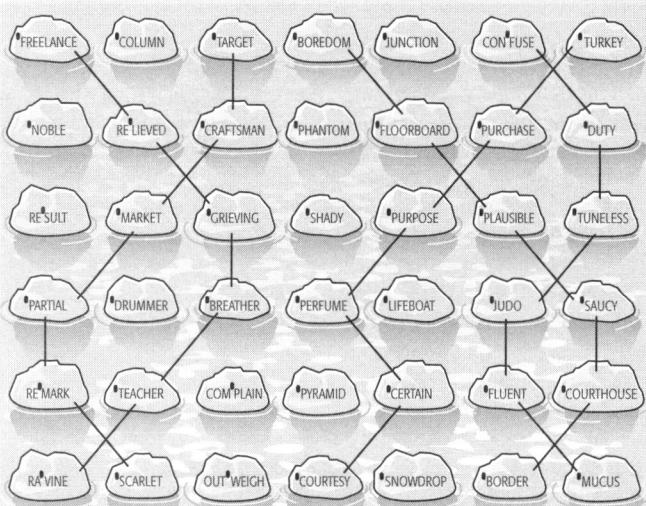

FREELANCE　COLUMN　TARGET　BOREDOM　JUNCTION　CON´FUSE　TURKEY
NOBLE　RE´LIEVED　CRAFTSMAN　PHANTOM　FLOORBOARD　PURCHASE　DUTY
RE´SULT　MARKET　GRIEVING　SHADY　PURPOSE　PLAUSIBLE　TUNELESS
PARTIAL　DRUMMER　BREATHER　PERFUME　LIFEBOAT　JUDO　SAUCY
RE´MARK　TEACHER　COM´PLAIN　PYRAMID　CERTAIN　FLUENT　COURTHOUSE
RA´VINE　SCARLET　OUT´WEIGH　COURTESY　SNOWDROP　BORDER　MUCUS

2

1　VOCABULARY

a

1　Are you 18 (years old)? This can often be seen in a pub where the legal age to drink alcohol is 18.
2　You drive. The name of a car/van hire company.
3　Free phone 0800 444 444. There is no charge for calling this number.
4　Light beer. Usually low-alcohol beer.
5　Night club. Evening entertainment venue.
6　Quick Bite. Snack bar where you can get something to eat quickly.
7　Better Books. The name of a bookshop.
8　Photo(graphic) shop. The name of a shop selling photographic equipment.
9　Drive through bank. Bank which you can use from your car.
10　Fish and chips. Restaurant or take-away selling fish and chips.

b

The corrected spellings are in bold.

> I **suppose** a **shopaholic** is someone whose life revolves around shopping; it's central to **their life** and starts to push out all other normal **activities**. These **people**, if they are not **actually** shopping, are **anxious** and **worried** or full of **excitement** based on the next day's shopping. Secondly, and **probably** the most **significant indicator** of a shopaholic, is when people don't **actually** get any **pleasure** from the goods after they've bought them. **Once** they leave the shop, they may never touch the goods; they hide them **away**. And, of **course**, most people carry on despite the growing **negative consequences** of credit card **debt**.

2　READING

a

1	paragraph 4	3	paragraph 3	5	paragraph 6
2	paragraph 1	4	paragraph 2	6	paragraph 5

b

1	chore (line 2)	7	a predisposition to (line 33)
2	perverse (line 3)	8	cheering (line 40)
3	habitat (line 8)	9	perimeter (line 43)
4	browsing (line 13)	10	aisles (line 45)
5	impulse purchasing (lines 19–20)	11	to and fro (line 60)
6	denizens (line 21)	12	subdued (line 70)

3　GRAMMAR

a

1	seeing	6	to inform	11	to tell
2	to recommend	7	to switch off	12	getting up
3	leaving	8	eating	13	going
4	to cancel	9	hearing	14	talking
5	making/to make	10	to eat		

b

1	in settling down	5	to leave	8	of getting
2	to send	6	of jumping	9	to get
3	of apologising	7	to alarm	10	to extend
4	of flying				

4　LISTENING

a

1	full stop	7	(forward) slash
2	comma	8	apostrophe
3	colon	9	inverted commas
4	semi-colon	10	(open) bracket
5	question mark	11	dash
6	exclamation mark		

b

If we read the newspapers or listen to the newscasters around the English-speaking world, we will quickly develop the impression that there is a World Standard English acting as a strongly unifying force among the vast range of variations which exist. There is a great deal of evidence to support this impression, it is true. However, it is misleading in several respects. A totally uniform, regionally neutral and unarguably prestigious variety does not yet exist.

Each country where English is a first language is aware of its linguistic identity and is anxious to preserve it from the influence of others. New Zealanders do not want to be Australians.

All other countries can be grouped into those which follow American English, those which follow British English and those where there is a mixture of influences.

One of the most noticeable features of this divided usage is spelling. In certain domains, such as computing and medicine, US spellings are becoming increasingly widespread, but we are a long way from uniformity.

c

If we read the newspapers // or listen to the newscasters around the English-speaking world *comma* // we will quickly develop the impression // that there is a World Standard English // acting as a strongly unifying force // among the vast range of variations which exist *full stop* // There is a great deal of evidence to support this impression *comma* // it is true *full stop* // However *comma* // it is misleading in several respects *full stop* // A totally uniform *comma* // regionally neutral // and unarguably prestigious variety does not yet exist *full stop* //

New paragraph Each country where English is a first language // is aware of its linguistic identity // and is anxious to preserve it from the influence of others *full stop* // New Zealanders do not want to be Australians *full stop* //

New paragraph All other countries can be grouped into those which follow American English *comma* // those which follow British English // and those where there is a mixture of influences *full stop* //

New paragraph One of the most noticeable features // of this divided usage is spelling *full stop* // In certain domains *comma* // such as computing and medicine *comma* // US spellings are becoming increasingly widespread *comma* // but we are a long way from uniformity *full stop* //

3

1 LISTENING

1   Indian nationalist movement
2   of great soul
3   non-violent confrontation/civil disobedience
4   October 2, 1869
5   chief minister
6   grocers and moneylenders
7   grocer
8   non-violence and vegetarianism
9   smoking
10 eating meat
11 telling lies
12 wearing Western clothes
13 13
14 law

15 London
16 South Africa
17 returned to India
18 direct political protest
19 Indian National Congress
20 British
21 hunger strike
22 improved status of the lowest classes
23 January 30, 1948

Mohandas Karamchand Gandhi, leader of the Indian nationalist movement and known in his later life as Mahatma, which means 'of great soul', was one of the greatest national leaders of the 20th century. His methods and philosophy of non-violent confrontation, or civil disobedience, not only led his own country to independence but influenced political activists of many persuasions throughout the entire world.

Gandhi was born in Porbandar, India, on October 2, 1869. Although his father was a chief minister for the Maharajah of Porbandar, the family came from the traditional caste of grocers and moneylenders. The name Gandhi means 'grocer'. His mother was a devout adherent of Jainism, a religion in which ideas of non-violence and vegetarianism are paramount. Gandhi stated that he was most influenced by his mother, whose life 'was an endless chain of fasts and vows'. When, in the company of boyhood friends, he secretly smoked, ate meat, told lies or wore Western clothing, he suffered intense feelings of guilt. These feelings forced him to make resolutions about his moral behaviour that were to stay with him for the rest of his life.

Married by arrangement at 13, Gandhi went to London to study law when he was 18. He was admitted to the bar in 1891 and for a while practised law in Bombay. From 1893 to 1914 he worked for an Indian firm in South Africa. During these years Gandhi's humiliating experiences of overt racial discrimination propelled him into agitation on behalf of the Indian community of South Africa. He assumed leadership of protest campaigns and gradually developed his techniques and tenets of non-violent resistance known as satyagraha, which literally means 'steadfastness in truth'.

Returning to India in January 1915, Gandhi soon became involved in labour organising. The massacre of Amritsar in 1919, in which troops fired on and killed hundreds of nationalist demonstrators, turned him to direct political protest. Within a year he was the dominant figure in the Indian National Congress, which he launched on a policy of non-cooperation with the British in 1920–22. Although total non-cooperation was abandoned, Gandhi continued his tactic of civil disobedience, organising protest marches against unpopular British measures, such as the salt tax of 1930 and boycotts of British goods.

Gandhi was repeatedly imprisoned by the British and resorted to hunger strikes as part of his civil disobedience. His final imprisonment came in 1942–44, after he had demanded total withdrawal of the British during World War II.

Together with his struggle for political independence, Gandhi fought to improve the status of the lowest classes of society, the casteless untouchables, whom he called harijans, 'children of God'. He was a believer in manual labour and simple living; he spun the thread and wove the cloth for his own garments and insisted that his followers do so too. He disagreed with those who wanted India to become an industrial country.

Gandhi was also tireless in his attempts to forge closer bonds between the Hindu majority and the numerous minorities of India. His greatest failure, in fact, was his inability to dissuade Indian Muslims, led by Muhammad Ali Jinnah, from creating a separate state, Pakistan. When independence was finally achieved in 1947, after negotiations in which he was a principal participant, Gandhi opposed the partition of the subcontinent with such intensity that he launched a mass movement against it. He was assassinated in Delhi on January 30, 1948, ironically by a Hindu fanatic who mistakenly thought his anti-partition sentiment was both pro-Muslim and pro-Pakistan.

2 PRONUNCIATION

Mohandas Karamchand Gandhi, leader⌣of the /j/Indian nationalist movement⌣and known⌣in his later life⌣as Mahatma, which means⌣'of great soul', was one⌣of the greatest national leaders⌣of the 20th century. His methods⌣and philosophy/j/of non-violent confrontation, or civil disobedience, not⌣only led his⌣own country to⌣/w/independence but⌣influenced political⌣ activists⌣of many persuasions throughout the/j/entire world.

3 READING

a

1 E   2 F   3 A   4 C   5 B   6 D

b

1 pelted (line 4)	5 languid (line 20)	8 lush (line 46)
2 shuffled (E)	6 soulful (line 21)	9 huddle (line D)
3 garlands (line 9)	7 ferns (line 32)	10 heaving (line 51)
4 clammy (line 14)		

4 GRAMMAR

a

1	a	defining	3	a	defining
	b	non-defining		b	non-defining
2	a	non-defining	4	a	non-defining
	b	defining		b	defining

b

1 in a defining clause when the relative pronoun is the object in its clause as in 4b in **a** – here *I've already spent the money I changed at the airport* would also be correct
2 to indicate that the information between the commas is non-essential and can be left out
3 in informal style
4 non-defining

c

1 O	3 O	5 S	7 S	9 O
2 S	4 O	6 O	8 S	10 O

d

The sentences which can be written without the relative pronoun are: 1, 3, 4, 6, 9, 10.

5 READING

1 *unbearable* is misused – if someone is unbearable, you can't stand them
2 *values* is misused – values means moral values; should be *valuables*
3 *flattening* should be *ironing/pressing*; *with pleasure* is the wrong phrase in the wrong place – should be *the chambermaid will be pleased to*
4 *to take advantage of* also means to seduce
5 *buried daily* suggests the same artists, etc., are buried again and again, day after day
6 combination of completely wrong (direct) translations and archaic language in *not to perambulate*, *hours of repose* and *boots of ascension*

7 *drop your trousers* also means to expose yourself to someone
8 *street walking* means prostitution
9 *execute* means kill when used with people
10 *to alarm* means to frighten; should be *alert*
11 *ass* in American English also means bottom/backside
12 *sends them in all directions* suggests bags are deliberately lost
13 *to have children* means to give birth
14 *to pass water* means to urinate; should be *has personally approved*

4

1 VOCABULARY

a

The phrasal verbs are given in order in their infinitive form.

see off	go to the airport/station to say goodbye to someone who is about to start a journey
run into	be faced with/meet (a problem)
get to	arrive at
pick up	go somewhere to collect someone in one's car, especially having previously arranged to do so
turn up	arrive
go off	leave
give up	stop doing something
bring on	cause something (unpleasant) to develop/happen
play up	cause problems, pain or difficulties
get on	become old
get over	return to one's usual mood after a surprise/shock
let on	reveal a secret
take on	undertake, agree to
pack in	do lots of things in a limited time
take up	use time
turn out	prove to be the case, become known

b

1 c   2 e   3 b   4 a   5 d

c

1 c   2 d   3 b   4 e   5 a

d

break into	verb + preposition
get through	verb + preposition
give off	verb + adverb particle
keep up	verb + adverb particle
put back	verb + adverb particle
fall through	verb + adverb particle
wear off	verb + adverb particle
play up	verb + adverb particle
come up	verb + adverb particle
drop off	verb + adverb particle

e

Prepositions: after, at, for, from, to, without.
Adverb particles: ahead, aside, away, forward, out.
Both prepositions and adverb particles: about, across, (a)round, by, down, in, near, outside, over.

f

1 without	3 (a)round	5 down
2 at	4 ahead	6 down

2 LISTENING

a

1	✗	3	✗	5	✓	7	✓	9	✓
2	✗	4	✓	6	✓	8	✓		

b

1 *could* make you anxious and depressed
2 *will* raise levels of brain serotonin almost instantly
3 *might* make you feel good in the short-term
4 *may* bring on forgetfulness, bad moods, confusion, inability to concentrate and sleep disturbance
5 *tend to be* happier
6 *may* boast extra brain enhancing power
7 *can* help lift your mood
8 *is likely to* affect your mental health

Got those mean moody blues?

What you eat can affect how you feel, think and act.

Let's look first at bad mood food.

Keep caffeine down to one or two cups of coffee a day. More could make you anxious and depressed.

A sugary snack will raise levels of brain serotonin almost instantly. This can give a short-term high, but beware of the let down. An hour or so after eating sugary foods, some people feel tired, unable to concentrate, even depressed.

Alcohol might make you feel good in the short-term but long-term is likely to lead to irritability, lethargy and depression. Research by Charles Lieber of the School of Medicine, New York, shows that the metabolism of alcohol in the body produces free radicals which may be released into the bloodstream. Damage to the brain tissue may bring on forgetfulness, bad moods, confusion, inability to concentrate and sleep disturbance.

Check for food allergies if you suffer persistent anxiety, tiredness or depression – malabsorption of vitamins may be responsible.

So which foods are feel-good enemies? Well, obviously, junk food, alcohol, caffeine, sugary cereals, snacks, sweets and drinks, and highly processed foods.

OK, so now let's take a look at good mood food.

Fruit and vegetable studies show people who eat more of these tend to be happier. Green leafy vegetables like asparagus, endive, spinach and kale contain an amino acid which can help improve intelligence, ease mental tiredness and fight depression.

Fish, which is vital to keep the brain in good working order, is a rich source of zinc and long chain essential fatty acids similar to those that form brain tissue. So is seafood which may boast extra brain enhancing power since it's also a source of dimethylaminoethanol – a super stimulant which gives a caffeine-like buzz without any ill effects.

Egg yolks and soya are good sources of choline, a B vitamin to help make chemicals that transmit messages between brain cells.

Bananas, turkey, chicken, fish, cooked dried beans, brewer's yeast, peanut butter, nuts and soya beans are all good sources of the amino acid tryptophan which can help lift your mood.

Try detoxifying. A build-up of toxins from a bad diet and pollution is likely to affect your mental health. Combine a diet high in organic fruit, vegetables, whole grains and plenty of water with a herbal detoxifying programme.

So which foods are feel-good friends?

Well, surprising for many people, chocolate. Then, of course, pasta and rice. Vegetables like red peppers, Brussel sprouts, spinach, kale, cabbage, kidney beans, lentils, pumpkin seeds and soya beans. Fish is important for our diet especially oysters, mackerel and herring. And while thinking about the sea, don't forget seaweed.

A chicken sandwich will give you a lift when you need it. Fruit, of course, especially bananas, kiwi fruit, figs, raspberries and strawberries.

Remember, oxygenating the blood via a short brisk walk is a great energiser and mood lifter.

3 GRAMMAR

1 will be able to
2 will have to
3 will have finished
4 leaves
5 will be living
6 were going to paint
7 Will (you) be staying/Are (you) staying
8 is going to be
9 are playing
10 will get
11 are staying/will be staying
12 Shall (I) order
13 won't go
14 shall have
15 is to speak/will speak
16 are to go/will go
17 will be taking

5

1 INFINITIVE OR -*ING* FORM?

1 They made us wait for one hour.
2 ✓
3 She persuaded me to choose the most expensive holiday.
4 He wanted me to meet him as soon as possible.
5 ✓
6 We are looking forward to hearing from you.
7 Would you mind opening the window?
8 ✓
9 Don't waste time making copies for all of us.
10 ✓
11 I don't remember seeing him before, do you?
12 I regret sending that letter; it caused a lot of embarrassment.
13 ✓
14 We'd like to learn golf this summer.
15 He stopped to have a break after driving non-stop for four hours.

2 SHORT AND LONG VOWELS

1	risen	3	pull	5	bird	7	boot	9	rug
2	forks	4	cart	6	slip	8	stalk	10	seat

3 SPELLING AND SOUNDS

a

/ɜː/ bird, fur, heard, her
/uː/ blue, choose, cruise, news, lose, shoe, through, use
/ɔː/ board, bored, bought, caught, door, pour, saw, short, talk, war
/iː/ each, piece, theme, tree

b

1	health	5	biscuit	8	temperature
2	doughnut	6	while	9	four
3	courtesy	7	rhyme	10	knowledge
4	snowdrop				

4 LINKING

1	/w/	/kʌm tuːwaɪslənd/	6	/j/	/pɑːs miːjəbɪskɪt/
2	/j/	/hiːjəraɪvd/	7	/j/	/baɪjɔːl əv ðəm/
3	/j/	/wiːjɑːnt gəʊɪŋ/	8	/j/	/aɪjəgriː/
4	/w/	/tuːwəndəhɑːf/	9	/w/	/truːwəfɒls/
5	/w/	/bluːwaɪz/	10	/w/	/hələʊwevrɪbɒdɪ/

5 RELATIVE CLAUSES

a

We can leave out the relative pronoun when it is the object of a defining clause.

b

1	O	3	S	5	O	7	O	9	O
2	S	4	S	6	S	8	O	10	O

6 TWO-PART PHRASAL VERBS

1 I'm going to pick her up from the station at 6pm.
2 We bumped into her in the supermarket.
3 He got over it quite quickly.
4 We'll take them on after Easter.
5 She seemed to frown on it.
6 I couldn't get it across to her that we only wanted to help.
7 We'll have to put it off.
8 I picked him out because he was so friendly.
9 He really looks like her.
10 We'll have to back her/him up on this one.

7 FUTURE FORMS

1 will/'ll finish
2 are going, won't see/won't be seeing
3 Shall (I) post, will (you) pass/will (you) be passing
4 will/'ll do
5 will/'ll have been
6 will/'ll be sitting
7 is to announce/will announce
8 is going to start/will be starting
9 Will (you) be dining/Are (you) dining
10 will be/is to be, will have to have fulfilled/will have to fulfil
11 Are (you) doing
12 shall submit/is to submit

8 ADJECTIVES FOLLOWED BY PREPOSITIONS

1	married to	5	involved in	8	typical of
2	commensurate with	6	adept at	9	liable to
3	qualified for	7	eligible for	10	applicable to
4	incompatible with				

6

1 VOCABULARY

1	f	4	k	7	d (also h)	10	b	13	n
2	g	5	l	8	m (also o)	11	c	14	a
3	e	6	j	9	o (also m)	12	i	15	h

2 READING

a

1 Features mentioned are: a calm and handsome stone façade, a pedimented porch, appropriate gardens, a gravel sweep between the front door and the street, lawns behind, a walled vegetable garden.
2 They spoilt it by adding a series of cramped leaking rooms at the back of the house.
3 They and their children will enjoy it for games, their bikes, camping and fighting.
4 They will knock out walls in the Victorian extension and repaint the rooms.
5 They think it has the right image for a successful couple.

b

1	pedimented (line 3)	5	crammed into (line 10)
2	gravel (line 4)	6	tannery (lines 13 and 14)
3	warren (line 7)	7	gagging (line 15)
4	battered (line 9)	8	set the seal upon (line 25)

3 VOCABULARY

a

1 b 2 g 3 f 4 h 5 d 6 c 7 a 8 e 9 i

b

1	droned on	5	crackled	8	squelched
2	sizzled/were sizzling	6	whimpering	9	moaning
3	chiming	7	swished	10	screeched
4	rattled				

4 GRAMMAR

1 was setting/set
2 was, has loved/had loved
3 had never been, was
4 felt/were feeling, had walked/had been walking
5 came out, were descending/descended
6 have been/had been, moved; were, had moved
7 have not developed
8 had not seen, saw
9 was reading, began
10 was watching/watched, was reading/read
11 had been sold/were sold, phoned
12 has been offered
13 Has (anybody) seen
14 didn't have/haven't had
15 had been/was, was going
16 have been studying
17 was lying
18 have eaten
19 did (you) leave
20 walked/was walking, had, had been, was

5 VOCABULARY

a

1 however
2 no sooner
3 in brief
4 first and foremost

b

1 in addition
2 on the contrary
3 consequently
4 with reference to
5 indeed
6 moreover
7 correspondingly
8 in conclusion
9 namely
10 hence
11 in spite of that
12 equally

6 READING

1 C   2 B   3 D   4 B   5 C   6 A

7

1 READING AND WRITING

2 will be talking/will talk/will give a talk
3 In addition
4 'ancient man'
5 climatic
6 geographic
7 supported/accompanied
8 will be available
9 limited
10 take place/start/begin
11 on
12 available
13 on Broadford
14 on the

2 GRAMMAR

a

| 1 | d | 3 | a | 5 | g | 7 | i | 9 | b |
| 2 | f | 4 | h | 6 | j | 8 | e | 10 | c |

b

Suggested answers:

3 (why don't you) open the window(?).
4 consult your doctor.
5 (why don't you) apply for it(?).
6 go on a diet.
7 (why don't you) try the new Mexican restaurant in town(?).
8 (why don't you) ask her out(?).

3 LISTENING

a

| 1 | b | 3 | e | 5 | c |
| 2 | d | 4 | f | 6 | a |

b

| 1 F | 3 T | 5 T | 7 F | 9 T |
| 2 F | 4 F | 6 T | 8 F | |

c

1 talking about the same thing in an annoying way
2 glasses (short for spectacles)
3 he thinks
4 is poor quality
5 honestly
6 mad
7 short for 'modern conveniences', i.e. modern gadgets
8 they certainly are a strange pair
9 wife
10 she has a lot of money
11 to keep him living a decent and honest life
12 someone who will never succeed
13 I can't remember his name (literally, what's his name)
14 fashionable
15 ten pounds
16 I'm sure
17 try to get all his money

DAN Did you see that bloke on the box last night, going on about how we've all become too materialistic and we've lost all our real values? It was a real laugh. I couldn't believe it.

CHRIS Yeah, I saw something like that. Was it some scruffy-looking bloke who lived in a really posh pad in the country?

DAN That's him, long hair, specs.

CHRIS What was he going on about?

DAN He reckons that anything that's modern is rubbish. Straight up, he's really off his head. Doesn't believe in having any mod cons in his house and he drives this clapped out old banger.

CHRIS Yeah, but isn't he Lord somebody or other? You can afford to be bonkers if you're a lord. It's all right depriving yourself of things when you know at the flick of a credit card you can have what you want.

DAN What's weird is he can't help making loads of money. He buys these old bangers right, 'cos he doesn't want any new-fangled sort of motor, and then it turns out they're worth a mint, you know, classic cars.

CHRIS Typical! Has he got any kids?

DAN Yeah. One's a sort of yuppy merchant banker type who lives in London and doesn't keep in touch with his dad at all. And the other's a drop-out in California. They're a right pair, as well.

CHRIS Was that classy looking women his missus? I can't imagine what a woman like that is doing with a weirdo like him. She looks as though she's worth a bob or two.

DAN Yeah, it seems she tries to keep him on the straight and narrow, but he's a lost cause. She doesn't need his money so I don't know why she stays with him. She's the daughter of whatsisname, you know, the bloke who owns all those trendy restaurants round the country.

CHRIS I know, those places where it's a tenner just to look at the menu.

DAN Anyway, going back to this bloke, he's got this new crackpot scheme to set up his own generator for electricity for their house and in any case get rid of most of the electrical stuff, like the fridge and what have you. Mind you, I got the impression his wife was about to throw a wobbly and I bet there'll be some serious falling out if he goes ahead with this one. She doesn't look the type to give up her luxuries easily. I can't blame her. It must be a nightmare living with a bloke like that.

CHRIS Well, she could always divorce him and take him to the cleaners. And of course, I'd be available for her!

DAN You'll be lucky. But what I'm saying is he wouldn't care. He's trying to get rid of all his loot, worldly possessions, all that kind of stuff.

CHRIS Praps we should write to him and say we could take some of it off his hands!

4 READING

1	B	3	A	5	D	7	D
2	C	4	D	6	B	8	C

8

2 VOCABULARY

1	ambition	6	loneliness
2	sympathy	7	delicacy
3	gentleness	8	modesty
4	dexterity	9	idealism
5	benevolence	10	innovation

3 GRAMMAR

a

1 fact   2 supposition   3 fact   4 fact   5 supposition

b

1   go, will (you) live/are (you) going to live/will (you) be living
2   would write, were/was
3   will pick (you) up, wait
4   are having, will call back
5   would like, will tell
6   used/were to use, would look
7   had not been, would have got
8   would have won, had not lost
9   would be, lived
10 had got, would not be
11 Would (it) be, came/come; Is (it)/Will (it) be, come
12 would appreciate, would confirm/confirmed
13 left, will have arrived; had left, would have arrived
14 had taken, would not have lost
15 want, will have to

4 VOCABULARY

a

2	outgrown	6	antisocial
3	Multilingual	7	Ex-husbands
4	underdogs	8	archenemies
5	apolitical		

b

1	b, f, h	3	e, j	5	a	7	c	9	c, f
2	d, g	4	d, i	6	a, h	8	a, i	10	e

5 PRONUNCIATION

a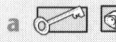

1	see	7	cash
2	shelf	8	chair
3	chin	9	sheep
4	which	10	ash
5	sheet	11	choose
6	mass	12	ship

b

The words make the letter O.

9

1 READING

a

1 D   2 A   3 E   4 F   5 C   6 B

b

1   albeit
2   bastion
3   *cheerleaders* lead the crowd in cheering (shouting loudly in encouragement) at a large public event
4   football played by girls is sissy and not to be taken seriously
5   caused by a strong reaction
6   in the wake of
7   *determination* and *bravery*
8   commentators
9   join together to form a whole; *make up* can also mean to put on make-up, to prepare by putting different things together, to invent and to become friends again
10 the journalist sees these girls as breaking new ground; *climb* has a connection with *pioneers* – these girls are the first girls to get into new territory (American football) and perhaps that is as difficult as climbing the highest mountain
11 geared towards
12 being tall and strong with big muscles is important
13 persuaded to appear on talk shows
14 it's an all-woman show so it's women talking to women
15 draw
16 get a strong feeling of excitement (adrenalin rush)
17 clothing/pads/helmet; *gear* can also refer to the system in engines which controls the rate at which the energy being used is converted into motion

2 GRAMMAR

2   the percussionist wouldn't fall asleep during the performance
3   sit next to the keyboard players than the string section
4   I had studied classical music at college
5   not play in a modern musical
6   she hadn't lost her music on the underground
7   this stage was made larger/to enlarge this stage/to make this stage larger
8   I had enough money to buy a new violin
9   Kate didn't take that job in Manchester
10 Eric retired; he's 73
11 Fiona didn't have to leave the company
12 to go home/we went home
13 my husband were/was rich and famous
14 I could remember the name of the theatre

3 VOCABULARY

a

1 unusable	5 unsatisfied/dissatisfied
2 priceless	6 exhaustive
3 economical	7 emotive/emotional
4 historic	

b

1 unusable: not able to be used
useless: serving no useful purpose
2 worthless: of no real value/use
priceless: very valuable
3 economic: concerned with economics
economical: not requiring a lot of money
4 historical: concerning past events
historic: important in history
5 unsatisfied: not satisfied/contented
dissatisfied: unhappy/displeased
6 exhausting: mentally or physically tiring
exhaustive: thorough and complete
7 emotional: concerned with the emotions
emotive: likely to make people feel strong emotions

4 LISTENING

1 T	3 F	5 T	7 F	9 T
2 T	4 F	6 F	8 F	10 F

DJ Everybody is out for a good time in a club – and different nationalities rarely agree what a good time is. In northern Europe the quality of the sound systems is exceptional, and more important than the appearance of the club. In Britain, as long as the club is full, everybody is happy. In Italy almost the exact opposite is true. When a new club is set up, designers are called in to model the look of the place, and the sound system is often the last thing to be attended to. Italian clubs favour leather sofas and gold trimmings but generally the music doesn't sound as good as it could. Of course there are exceptions, like Movida in Rimini.

A club like the Escape, in Amsterdam – a converted cinema, which is a great club and looks really distinctive although it isn't meticulously designed – couldn't happen in Italy.

One of my favourite cities is Stockholm – people are so open, friendly and liberated. I think generally northern Europeans are more mentally open, southern Europeans more emotionally open. The south is more open to 'house' music – 'happy' house music – because it reflects this difference, and it fits better with the sun and the feeling of openness. Techno music works better in industrialised areas because it sounds more mechanistic. And then, in Britain, you get things like drum'n'bass and jungle, which are more turned on to the adrenalin of living in a huge city – more frenetic, and probably less likely to penetrate completely in Italy, even if drum'n'bass does have a bit more of a following now.

France is getting more exciting now. They've got some great DJs. But in organisational terms, Germany is still really together – perhaps because the techno scene in Berlin has been going for quite some time, or because of their quite liberated attitudes. There are some incredible clubs in Berlin which I couldn't imagine seeing anywhere else and in Frankfurt there's this place called The Tunnel, a subterranean venue that's about three kilometres long – in the centre of town!

5 VOCABULARY

1 d	5 j	8 e
2 i	6 c	9 g (also i)
3 h (also g)	7 f (also b, g)	10 a (also d)
4 b (also j)		

6 READING AND EDITING

3 ✓	8 all	13 to
4 about	9 it	14 own
5 been	10 ✓	15 of
6 also	11 so (first one)	16 ✓
7 ✓	12 so	17 ✓

7 PRONUNCIATION

a

1 practise	5 swallow	8 announced
2 thanked	6 frequent	9 dreadful
3 school	7 quickly	10 marched
4 fifths		

c

1 /fleɪms/	5 /tɑːsks/	8 /sɪksθs/
2 /spiːk/	6 /kræʃ/	9 /greɪtɪd/
3 /twentɪ/	7 /helpt/	10 /skrætʃ/
4 /pʌntʃt/		

10

1 PAST TENSES AND THE PRESENT PERFECT

1 was, has played/has been playing
2 felt/were feeling, had been playing/had played
3 were, had moved
4 hadn't been, saw
5 had been sold/were sold, got
6 has made
7 had been talking/was talking, realised
8 have been
9 was playing, jumped
10 went out, were trying
11 have not seen
12 Has (anybody) seen/Did (anybody) see

2 LINKERS

1 Besides → Because/Since
2 ✓
3 Because → Because of
4 so → such
5 yet → so (that)
6 ✓
7 For conclusion → In conclusion
8 Despite of → Despite/In spite of
9 ✓
10 such → so

3 READING AND EDITING

3	being	8	✓	13	small
4	up	9	just	14	✓
5	as	10	their	15	every
6	✓	11	the (second one)	16	of
7	than	12	being		

4 CONDITIONAL FORMS

1 had booked, would have got
2 train/are training, will be able to
3 Were (Jane) to be asked, would accept
4 pay/have paid, will forward
5 would be working, had come; will be working, came
6 is, means
7 had not turned up, would (you) have waited
8 travel, get
9 Would (it) be, called
10 has taken, will have arrived; had taken/took, would have arrived
11 would like, will tell
12 are working/going to work, will go/am going

5 PREFIXES AND SUFFIXES

1	dissatisfied	5	immature	8	inhospitable
2	illegal	6	dishonest	9	discouraging
3	non-conformist	7	unwritten	10	irreproachable
4	unfaithful				

6 *WISH, IF ONLY, WOULD RATHER, IT'S TIME*

1 we went home/to go home
2 sit near the stage than in the circle
3 the show would start
4 the circus would come to Glasgow
5 John had time to help us
6 not spend a summer's day watching a video
7 the play weren't/wasn't so boring
8 it would stop raining
9 he wouldn't dance like that
10 my father had stopped smoking years ago
11 to have lunch/for lunch/we had lunch
12 we had had the tickets posted
13 the language of the play hadn't been modernised
14 Christine didn't have to do two shows a day
15 Suzanne had her violin repaired

7 ORDER OF ADJECTIVES

1 fascinating thick 17th-century faded vellum *manuscript*
2 exciting new colourful Brazilian dance *routine*
3 highly successful huge American vegetarian restaurant *chain*
4 politically incorrect traditional British fairy *story*
5 accurate detailed computer colour *analysis*
6 overly formal wordy 70s legal *document*
7 useful A3 transparent plastic *folder*
8 ornate hexagonal mahogany theatre *box*
9 realistic epic black and white German horror *film*
10 revolting avant-garde pinkish interior *decor*

11

1 VOCABULARY

a and b

1 e – in the end, illegal dealings will not benefit you
2 j – the person with financial control makes the decisions
3 f – a person with a very nice side and a very bad side to their character
4 a – take money reserved for one thing and spend it on another
5 b – trying to do something and, if it's wrong, trying again
6 h – the legal system can be ridiculous
7 c – without having a drop of alcohol
8 g – to persuade someone
9 i – the police
10 d – mysterious, like in old films or novels

2 READING

1 C   2 G   3 F   4 J   5 H   6 I   7 A   8 D

3 VOCABULARY

a

1	d + iii	4	c + x	7	h + vii	10	g + v
2	e + iv	5	f + i	8	j + ix		
3	i + viii	6	b + ii	9	a + vi		

b

1	kept/went	5	get	9	get
2	picked	6	are/are getting	10	go
3	settle	7	come		
4	miss	8	come/coming		

4 GRAMMAR

a

1	no necessity	5	probability	8	necessity
2	inability	6	possibility	9	obligation
3	inadvisability	7	unwillingness	10	probability
4	probability				

b

1	pleasure	5	contemplation	8	indulgence
2	presumption	6	irritation	9	apologising
3	criticism	7	annoyance	10	speculation
4	resignation				

c

I'm very sorry to hear about your accident. I **can't** believe that the driver tried to drive off and leave you. If the policeman hadn't followed him he **might** never have been caught.

Jane told me that you're thinking of dropping the charges; Jenny you **mustn't** do that. It's important that people like him don't get away with it. He **must** be hoping you won't take it too seriously but honestly you **could/might** have been killed! I know you **didn't have to** stay in hospital long but that's not the point.

You **should/must** employ a good solicitor; you **needn't/mustn't** worry about the cost. You are eligible for legal aid as you are a student. You **must/might** think I've got a cheek telling you what to do but it's not like that. I just **can't/couldn't** stand by and say and do nothing.

Could/Can you let me know what you decide to do? And of course I'll stand by you whatever you decide.

5 VOCABULARY

a

1 jury
2 usher
3 witness box
4 judge
5 public gallery
6 lawyer (for the defence or prosecution)
7 clerk of the court
8 the dock
9 defendant

b

1 of	5 of	9 for	
2 to	6 in, of	10 under	
3 for	7 in		
4 in	8 out of		

Sentences 4 and 7 can be written without a preposition.

12

1 READING

1 entering/in	9 not	17 terms
2 in	10 whose	18 for
3 gave	11 like	19 which/what
4 scale	12 but	20 stems/comes
5 place/put/rank	13 us	21 attempt/effort
6 Everyone/Everybody	14 such	22 part
7 being	15 turn	23 reluctance
8 question	16 with	24 to

2 VOCABULARY

a

1 h	3 e	5 d	7 c	9 b
2 i	4 a	6 j	8 g	10 f

b

1 grain (also hint)	5 round	8 hint (also dash)
2 flash	6 pile (also load)	9 item
3 dash (also hint)	7 stretch	10 load
4 handful		

3 LISTENING

1 holidays
2 foreign travel available to all but the poor
3 it's an offshore outpost/it's not centrally positioned
4 spare capacity
5 finance industry will suffer
6 green belt land
7 wildfowl and wading birds
8 Water Aven/plant
9 sewage and sludge plant
10 'noise footprint' (and) flight path
11 no greater noise
12 no more car parks

13 3 rapid rail links
14 one sixth of transport fuel
15 natural habitats move 80km north per decade
16 world reduction of carbon emissions by 60–80%
17 reduction of 20% by 2010
18 3% of global carbon emissions
19 2
20 10
21 30
22 fuel/travel rationing

Air travel is rising by 4 per cent a year and London Heathrow's new fifth terminal, T5, is urgently needed. Most of the extra demand each year is for holidays. Never before have so many British people travelled abroad so much. What used to be exclusively a rich man's pleasure is now available to all but the poor: weddings on a beach in the Seychelles, families flying to Florida, winter breaks in the sun.

Despite being an offshore outpost, London is the biggest airport in Europe. Amsterdam, Paris and Frankfurt are bidding to overtake it. All have plenty of spare capacity, eager to take over any extra business if Britain lets slip. The City fears the knock-on effect to their global finance industry if London no longer remains the key entry airport to Europe. All these are good reasons why the decision to build T5 is inevitable.

Friends of the Earth have raised local environmental issues. T5 will be the largest ever structure built on green belt land. The site is a wetland that is one of London's best for wildfowl and wading birds. As ever, there has been a last minute discovery of a rare species, this time a plant called a Water Aven. The site sounds like a rural paradise. In fact this rare 'wetland' is a sewage and sludge plant, hardly an idyllic picnic spot.

The more serious challenge has been from local residents, the 300,000 dwellings deafened within the 'noise footprint' of the airport and others in the flight path. The British Airport Authority now guarantee there will be no greater noise, that there will be no further car parks, and, most important of all, there will be three new rapid rail links to cut down car use. All that is little consolation to the wretched sufferers who live nearby. Yet, however much we pity local residents, we all want to fly.

But then, we also all want to breathe – and by any standards, an airport is an environmental calamity. Air travel accounts for one sixth of fuel used for transport. Global warming is here: few dispute it now, with natural habitats shifting 80km north per decade. To halt it the Intergovernmental Panel on Climate Change say the world needs to reduce carbon emissions by 60–80 per cent.

Britain has promised a reduction of 20 per cent by 2010 – and the UK only contributes 3 per cent to global carbon emissions. Since air travel is only a small part of that, why worry about a bigger airport? Well, one person's round trip from London to Florida uses up around half the total annual carbon emission allowance for each person for all purposes, according to the IPCC recommendations, if the world is to survive.

Strangely, air travel is not counted into each country's inventory of greenhouse gas emissions, as no-one could decide how to apportion it. America is reluctant to reduce any emissions at all, though every American consumes double the energy of every Briton, 10 times each Chinese and 30 times each Indian. In the face of that, it's tempting to despair. Why should any country worry about a little bit more here and there, while the Americans guzzle on regardless?

But some day soon we will have to ration energy use, in planes and cars. There will come a time when suddenly the world is frightened by disasters into allowing politicians to do what must be done. Will we find a socially acceptable way to ration energy, or will the rich take it all?

Here is one scheme some environmentalists have put forward. If as a nation we set a limit to the total number of air miles flown, or indeed to the number of car miles driven, we could issue a ration to every citizen. Those who don't want to use their flying or driving ration could sell their quota on the open market. The rich would scramble to buy, the poor to sell if they wanted to, if the price was enticing enough. Rations would become very valuable and it would lead to a healthy redistribution of wealth that had nothing to do with taxation.

4 GRAMMAR

2 is believed (that) the increase in air travel is due to holidaymakers
3 is being dealt with
4 had already been sent the results of the tests by the doctor
5 were seen entering the main building
6 was made to apologise by her parents
7 is thought to have gone abroad last night
8 is said to have been a disagreement between the surgeon and the theatre sister
9 with the press has been put off twice now
10 should be made payable to The Clinic
11 been fed by his mother, the baby went to sleep
12 for money and possessions can be called 'greed'

5 VOCABULARY

1	dressed	7	shirty
2	veil	8	hat
3	cloaked	9	shoes
4	skirted	10	coated
5	button	11	socked
6	collared	12	buttonholed

13

1 READING

2	G	4	A	6	B
3	E	5	I	7	H

2 GRAMMAR

1 Antarctica (Note: *The* Arctic isn't a true continent, but a combination of frozen ocean and islands belonging to other continents.)
2 The Thames (Note: Here *Th* in *Thames* is pronounced /t/.)
3 The Philippines
4 Egypt
5 The Andes
6 The Gobi Desert
7 Ankara
8 The Amazon
9 Sydney
10 Wall Street
11 The Atlantic
12 Everest
13 The Sun
14 Lake Titicaca (It's also the largest lake in South America and is 3,812m above sea-level.)
15 California

3 LISTENING

a

1	T	3	F	5	T	7	F
2	T	4	T	6	F	8	T

Have you ever had a day when you thought you would have been better off staying in bed? At breakfast, your toast slides off your plate and lands on the floor, butter-side down. Getting dressed you spend ages rummaging through a drawer full of socks and fail to find a single pair that matches. At the supermarket you queue up at the checkout only to find yourself going nowhere, while the queue next to yours zooms through. If you have always suspected that such vexations aren't flukes, but the manifestations of a cosmic law, I have good news for you, or bad, depending on your point of view. I can confirm that your suspicions are correct: Murphy's Law – if something can go wrong, it will – is built into our universe.

For years, the attitude of most scientists towards Murphy's Law, or Sod's Law to some, has been to dismiss it as some silly urban myth. But over the past two years I've discovered that it's the scientists who have got it wrong.

Toast usually will fall butter-side down, and it's easy to explain. A simple experiment will show you what happens. Get a paperback book and put it face-up on the table. Now slowly push it over the edge to simulate toast sliding off a plate. As it goes over the edge, the book starts to tip over and spin. The trouble is, it doesn't spin fast enough to come face-up again by the time it hits the floor. Barring a lucky bounce, the book or toast will end up face-down more or less every time. It's simply a product of the forces of gravity and friction.

The trouble with so many other examples of Murphy's Law, like why there is always a spoon left in the bottom of the washing-up bowl, is that they're anecdotal, and so difficult to analyse convincingly. Even so, I've found many which can be analysed, like the one about why the other queue usually moves faster than yours. Believe it or not, an entire branch of applied mathematics is devoted to the behaviour of queues and what they've found is that although the queues, say in a supermarket, are all subject to random delays, on average they'll tend to move at the same rate.

Many people will argue that that isn't their personal experience. They find the other queue does move more quickly. But the key word here is 'average'. When we go to the supermarket, we're not interested in averages – we just want our queue to be the fastest on that particular trip. And in that case, even if all the queues are exactly the same length, the chances that ours will suffer fewer random delays than both our neighbours is just one in three – two-thirds of the time, one or other of our neighbours will do better and finish before us.

Another good one is why socks so rarely stay in pairs. Murphy's Law of Odd Socks – if an odd sock can be created, then it will be – turns out to be another demonstration of the cussedness of probability. Imagine a drawer containing nothing but complete pairs of socks. Now suppose one sock goes missing, don't worry about which one, where, or how. Clearly you just created an odd sock left behind in the drawer. Now suppose a second sock goes missing. It could be the odd sock created last time, but it's far more likely to be from one of the many unbroken pairs still in the drawer. The chances are thus heavily stacked towards this second sock creating yet another odd sock in the drawer. And so the process goes on. Probability theory confirms Murphy's Law of Odd Socks in mathematical detail.

In fact, many other things can also be explained in a scientific way – things like why string so often gets into knots and why the place you want to get to is so frequently on the awkward division between two pages on the map or right on one edge. They all follow some mathematical theorem or the laws of probability. In the case of the map, simple geometry is the key.

Well, I don't know if you now feel relieved that it's all beyond your control. Perhaps you're disappointed there isn't something more mysterious going on. Either way I hope I've shed some light on a phenomenon we all experience in our daily lives, usually at the least convenient moments! Thank you very much.

b

1	d	3	c	5	g	7	j	9	f
2	h	4	i	6	b	8	a	10	e

4 VOCABULARY

1 This is really irritating/annoying/worrying me.
2 Do something even though it is dangerous.
3 We made a good profit/benefited from the deal.
4 It's not good manners.
5 No deal./That's not acceptable.
6 That's enough./That's OK.
7 I can't manage without that.
8 She swindled/cheated me out of £50.
9 I'm really tired/exhausted.
10 Do whatever you want.

5 PRONUNCIATION

a

1	omelette	6	different	11	awfully
2	evening	7	usually	12	aspirin
3	business	8	restaurant	13	extraordinary
4	marriage	9	secretary	14	separate
5	every	10	Wednesday		

b

1	'omelette	6	'different	11	'awfully
2	'evening	7	'usually	12	'aspirin
3	'business	8	'restaurant	13	e'xtraordinary
4	'marriage	9	'secretary	14	'separate
5	'every	10	'Wednesday		

6 VOCABULARY

1 A stamen   B petal   C stem   D leaf
2 A branch   B trunk   C roots   D twig
  E bud   F bark
3 A skin/peel/rind   B pith   C pip   D segment
4 A kernel   B shell
5 A shell   B white   C yolk

14

1 READING

a

1 F   2 E   3 A   4 C

b

1 someone addicted to information
2 someone addicted to alcohol
3 someone addicted to chocolate
4 someone addicted to work
5 mail you receive which you do not want and is no good to you, like advertising blurb
6 fast food

2 GRAMMAR

a

1 is the demand for Internet services that many people are finding it difficult to get on-line
2 I realised how long it would take, I would never have started

3 when we went to the USA did we realise the extent of PC use
4 has Jane changed her lifestyle but she has also abandoned her old friends
5 did we suspect that she had been neglecting her children
6 had we got new computers than all the students enrolled for the IT course
7 was I told how to use it
8 comes the waiter
9 jumped the boy
10 does his brother

b

1 Scarcely *had I entered* the room when the butler appeared.
2 ✓
3 ✓
4 Not only *does the computer make you* tired, but it also wastes a lot of time.
5 ✓
6 'So *would I.*'
7 Down the stairs *she tumbled* like a rag doll. (Note: inversion is not possible with a pronoun)
8 *There sits* the designer, Vivienne Westwood. (Or no inversion if you want to keep the continuous form: *The designer Vivienne Westwood is sitting there.*)
9 ✓
10 ✓

3 READING AND VOCABULARY

1	A	3	A	5	B	7	C	9	A
2	C	4	D	6	B	8	D	10	C

4 VOCABULARY

a

1	c	3	j	5	a	7	i	9	e
2	h	4	b	6	g	8	d	10	f

b

1	dumbstruck	6	scrapbooks
2	getaway	7	smokescreen
3	telling-off	8	terror-stricken
4	bodyguards/a bodyguard	9	cut-throat
5	weak-kneed	10	makeshift

15

1 READING AND VOCABULARY

1	C	5	B	9	D	13	A	17	A
2	D	6	C	10	C	14	C	18	C
3	D	7	B	11	B	15	D		
4	A	8	A	12	A	16	B		

2 VOCABULARY

1	in	3	on	5	with	7	on	9	with
2	in	4	about	6	from	8	at	10	from

3 LISTENING

1 intimate relationships
2 0–45cm
3 close physical contact; visual distortion when very close
4 'personal distance'
5 45cm–1.2m
6 moderate level of voice; only odours like perfume detectable
7 'social distance'
8 impersonal or formal relationships
9 1.2m–2.1m or 2.1m–3.6m
10 'public distance'
11 speaker to an audience
12 3.6m–7.6m or more than 7.6m

Personal space has a number of different definitions depending on the distances we feel comfortable with for different situations. At the individual level, we generally reserve what is referred to as 'intimate distance' for close intimate relationships. Research finds this to be between 0 to 45cm. It often involves close physical contact and, when looking at someone, visual distortion the closer we get. This distance is too close for acquaintances, and people can be seen to be withdrawing in certain social situations when the distance between them narrows to this amount.

The distance we generally use for conversing with family and friends and business colleagues is called 'personal distance' and has been found to be between 45cm and 1.2m. We use a moderate level of voice, and unlike in intimate relationships, at the further levels of personal distance the only odours detectable are those deliberately displayed such as perfumes and after-shave lotions.

'Social distance' may be seen at times of impersonal transactions, such as purchasing something in a shop. It involves more formal contacts where status and decorum are retained. It can occur at a close range, found to be between 1.2 and 2.1m, or at a far range, between 2.1 and 3.6m.

'Public distance' is used where a speaker addresses an audience and could be between 3.6 and 7.6m in some situations and further than 7.6 in others.

4 GRAMMAR

a

1 She said she felt very uncomfortable talking to John then because he was standing too close.
2 She said (that) if they had observed people's behaviour in cities, they would have got very different results.
3 She said city dwellers had developed finely honed skills to deal with crowds.
4 He said (that) unless they adapted to the culture, they would find it difficult to get on there.
5 He said I/you/we might be able to avoid eye contact by reading a book.
6 He asked (me/us) if people shook/shake hands with each other in Japan.
7 She asked (me/us) what people did/do in my country when they met/meet for the first time.
8 She asked if I/we could meet them the next day.
9 She told me not to look at her like that. I was making her feel guilty.
10 She asked me/you/him/her/us/them to open the window.

b

1 me not to take the underground late at night
2 me to wear a dark suit as it was quite a formal meeting

3 (that) he had made a mistake
4 (that) there would be two more for dinner
5 (that) it would cost £5,000
6 me to go to the opening
7 (that) she hadn't moved it
8 me to study sociology
9 (that) Philip and I try/tried the new Italian restaurant
10 me/us not to sit next to Pat as she was/is such a bore

5 VOCABULARY

a

1	etymology	11	sociology
2	astrology	12	seismology
3	arachnology	13	geology
4	psychology	14	lepidopterology
5	vulcanology	15	campanology
6	oceanology	16	toxicology
7	horology	17	mythology
8	entomology	18	meteorology
9	archaeology	19	theology
10	phrenology	20	graphology

b

archae'ology, a'strology, campa'nology, ento'mology, ety'mology, ge'ology, gra'phology, ho'rology, lepidopte'rology, meteo'rology, my'thology, ocea'nology, phre'nology, psy'chology, seis'mology, soci'ology, the'ology, toxi'cology, vulcan'ology

16

1 MODAL VERBS

1	couldn't	6	couldn't	11	must
2	should	7	don't have to	12	can't
3	needn't	8	might	13	can
4	Could	9	needn't have gone	14	shouldn't
5	could	10	didn't need to go	15	might

2 PREPOSITIONS

1	out of	3	of	5	under	7	in (favour) of
2	for	4	of	6	to	8	in

3 WORD STRESS

1	le'gality	5	crimi'nology	9	'prosecutor
2	judge'mental	6	fo'rensics	10	accu'satory
3	'precedent	7	eligi'bility		
4	confis'cation	8	de'fendant		

4 THREE-PART PHRASAL VERBS

1	put in for	6	get on/along with
2	lived up to/came up to	7	went in for
3	put (it) down to	8	looking forward to
4	puts up with	9	put (you) down for
5	catch up with	10	is in for

5 THE PASSIVE

1 Tests are being run on the new machinery this week.
2 High-quality electronic goods are produced in Korea.
3 The application form must be received before the end of the month.
4 He was thought to have left the country.
5 She was made to take another driving test.
6 It is expected that the winner will be announced next Monday.
7 She is believed to be a talented musician.
8 Young men are said to be the worst drivers.
9 I was asked to be waiting in the foyer.
10 We were allowed to enter the palace.

6 INVERSION

1 you need any further information, please do not hesitate to contact us
2 do his ministers
3 does Nicki run a successful company, but she also manages to look after her four children
4 had the concert started than there was an electrical fault and the lights went out
5 did I imagine that anyone would object
6 stood a Ming vase
7 had the opera started when the principal singer fainted
8 have I had such a good time
9 was his embarrassment that he left the room
10 did we realise that he was her father

7 COUNTABLE AND UNCOUNTABLE NOUNS

1	ball	5	dab	9	roll/reel
2	blade	6	school/shoal	10	sheet/pad
3	bunch	7	herd		
4	clove	8	pint/barrel/glass		

8 COMPOUND WORDS

1	smokescreen	6	dumbstruck/gobsmacked
2	bodyguard	7	latecomers
3	day-trippers/holidaymakers	8	getaway
4	scrapbook	9	weak-kneed/feeble-minded
5	voice-activated	10	makeshift

Phonetic symbols

LONG VOWELS

iː sheep /ʃiːp/	ɑː farm /£fɑːm/ /$fɑːrm/	ɔː horse /£hɔːs/ /$hɔːrs/	uː shoe /ʃuː/	ɜː bird /£bɜːd/ /$bɜːrd/

SHORT VOWELS

ɪ ship /ʃɪp/	e head /hed/	æ hat /hæt/	ʌ cup /kʌp/	(Br)ɒ sock /£sɒk/	ʊ foot /fʊt/	ə above /ə'bʌv/	(Am)ɚ mother /$'mʌð·ɚ/

DIPHTHONGS (two vowel sounds together)

eɪ day /deɪ/	aɪ eye /aɪ/	ɔɪ boy /bɔɪ/	aʊ mouth /maʊθ/	(Br)əʊ nose /£nəʊz/	(Am)oʊ nose /$noʊz/	(Br)ɪə ear /£ɪəʳ/	(Br)ea hair /£heaʳ/	(Br)ʊə pure /£pjʊəʳ/

CONSONANTS

voiceless	p pen /pen/	t town /taʊn/	k cat /kæt/	f fish /fɪʃ/	θ think /θɪŋk/	s say /seɪ/	ʃ she /ʃiː/	tʃ cheese /tʃiːz/
voiced	b book /bʊk/	d day /deɪ/	g give /gɪv/	v very /'ver·ɪ/	ð the /ðə/	z zoo /zuː/	ʒ vision /vɪʒn/	dʒ jump /dʒʌmp/
	l look /lʊk/	r run /rʌn/	j yes /jes/	w we /wiː/	m moon /muːn/	n name /neɪm/	ŋ sing /sɪŋ/	h hand /hænd/